Stock Market Investing for Beginners

Simple Proven Strategies and Tactics to Become a Profitable Intelligent Investor by Getting Hold of the Tricks Behind the Trade Toward Success and Fortune

By

David Reese

Table of Content

Introduction 6

Chapter 1: 8

30 Lessons to Get Started with the Right Mindset and Understanding 8

Chapter 2: 36

Three ways to jump start your investing experience ... 36

Chapter 3: 45

What is the stock market? 45

Chapter 4: 56

What is an IPO? 56

Chapter 5: 60

What are mutual funds and 60

how to use them 60

Chapter 6: 63

Where to buy and sell stocks 63

Chapter 7: 68

Is it worth it to invest in stocks? 68

Chapter 8: 80

Investing basics – common mistakes 80

Chapter 9: 91

How to choose a good 91

stock to invest in... 91

Chapter 10: 100

How to invest big sums of money 100

Chapter 11: 103

How to decide if it is time 103

to buy or sell a share 103

Chapter 12: 131

Indicators to look for 131

before investing...131

Chapter 13: 138

How to diversify your investment...................................138

Conclusion 146

© Copyright 2018 by **David Reese** - All rights reserved.

The following eBook is reproduced below with the goal of providing information that is as accurate and reliable as possible. Regardless, purchasing this eBook can be seen as consent to the fact that both the publisher and the author of this book are in no way experts on the topics discussed within and that any recommendations or suggestions that are made herein are for entertainment purposes only. Professionals should be consulted as needed prior to undertaking any of the action endorsed herein.

This declaration is deemed fair and valid by both the American Bar Association and the Committee of Publishers Association and is legally binding throughout the United States.

Furthermore, the transmission, duplication, or reproduction of any of the following work including specific information will be considered an illegal act irrespective of if it is done electronically or in print. This extends to creating a secondary or tertiary copy of the work or a recorded copy and is only allowed with the express written consent from the Publisher. All additional right reserved.

The information in the following pages is broadly considered a truthful and accurate account of facts and as such, any inattention, use, or misuse of the information in question by the reader will render any resulting actions solely under their purview. There are no scenarios in which the publisher or the original author of this work can be in any fashion deemed liable for any hardship or damages that may befall them after undertaking information described herein.

Additionally, the information in the following pages is intended only for informational purposes and should thus be thought of as universal. As befitting its nature, it is presented without assurance regarding its prolonged validity or interim quality. Trademarks that are mentioned are done without written consent and can in no way be considered an endorsement from the trademark holder.

Introduction

Congratulations on downloading *Stock Market Investing for Beginners: Simple Proven Strategies and Tactics to Become a Profitable Intelligent Investor by Getting Hold of the Tricks Behind the Trade Toward Success and Fortune* and thank you for doing so. The world of stock investing is growing increasingly chaotic and downloading this book is the first step you can take towards actually doing something about it. The first step is also always the easiest, however, the information you find in the following chapters is so important to take to heart, as they are not concepts that can be put into action immediately. If you file them away for when they are really needed, however, then when the time comes to actually use them, you will be glad you did.

To that end, the following chapters will discussthe primary preparedness principles that you will need to consider if you ever hope to realistically be successful in the investing world. This means you will want to consider the quality of your stocks including the potential issues raised by their current value, how they can be best utilized in an emergency to drive in quick cash, and how to operate with them properly.

With shares out of the way, you will then learn everything you need to know about investing a wide variety of markets including stocks, forex, and commodities. Rounding out the three primary requirements for successful investing, you will then learn about crucial risk management principles and what they will mean for you. Finally, you will learn how investing is the quickest way to reach financial freedom.

There are plenty of books on this subject on the market, so thanks again for choosing this one! Every effort was made to ensure it is full of as much useful information as possible. Please enjoy!

Chapter 1:

30 Lessons to Get Started with the Right Mindset and Understanding

Because of the continuous difficulties that have involved international stock exchanges in the recent months, many have begun to ask themselves the fateful question: "Is investing in shares still the best strategy to multiply my savings?"

The financial markets in general can be an extraordinary opportunity: not only stocks but also cryptocurrencies and forex can give great satisfaction even if, however, it is necessary to have a preparation before going into rash choices.

In this chapter, we will go deep into the subject and discover the 30 golden lessons that every investor should know before entering the stock market.

1. Easy money is like Santa Claus: it does not exist!

Whoever promises to quintuple your assets without sweating is no more than a seller of smoke. Investing in the stock market is not a joke and to achieve the investment goals you have, set yourself to avoid risky securities and focus on something more stable, lasting, and profitable. In the recipe for success, in addition to a serious knowledge of the stock markets, there is also the sentimental component. For those investing, there is no room for panic; instead, you need a lot of patience and even a bit of luck.

2. Gold and cash do not give interest

Everyone knows that cash does not disappear, but after the bizarre manoeuvres of the European Central Bank (which brought negative returns on the single currency), we can be even more certain that investing in cash does not create any interest. Everyone's dream is to be able to accumulate the amount of money enough to enjoy a quiet retirement, but as the closer it gets to the time x, the small investor tends to panic. This results in reckless choices to invest in cash or in commodities such as gold, which, although it proves to be more stable than fiat, cannot hold the same value forever. Just think that in the last lustre, the value of the most precious metal fell by 34.8%.

3. The ingredients for a winning strategy

One of the main factors of success on the stock exchange is sentiment: patience, foresight, and prudence are the three basic ingredients of winning strategies, but it is also true that a little risk never hurts.

If the money we have invested on a certain stock does not return, you should look around and find some slightly riskier but profitable activity, with the hope that an important injection of money into the markets can restart the economy by stimulating productivity and development.

4. Establish investment goals

Before starting to invest and embarking on a challenging and long path, you must have a clear mindset of where you want to go. It depends on personal aspirations, on the trust that one has for himself, and on many other factors. However, the main choice is between protecting capital and making it grow. Under certain conditions, the stock exchange also lends itself to the speculative approach. One who wants to start could also establish concrete objectives such as buying a good or a service. In any case, the rule is always the same: to understand where you want to arrive.

5. Establish the degree of risk tolerance

This is probably the most important phase. The stock market is in fact extremely varied and allows numerous approaches, from the prudent and static to the dynamic and courageous.

This is why it is always good to establish one's degree of tolerance. Based on this decision, further choices will be made until the real investment is realized. Investor profiles depend on personal characteristics and their economic situation. If you are a simple worker, do not sail in gold and maybe for those who invest their savings of a lifetime, it is good to give up any speculative ambitions. The degree of tolerance determines the risk that you intend to run and the strategy that will be adopted later.

6. Studying

The information issue should not be forgotten. The stock market is complex and structurally risky, so we need to be cautious. The risk is to lose capital in a short period of time. Therefore, it is necessary to undertake a training course that confers at least the theoretical tools. The topic of the study should consist of both the investment modalities, how it is invested, and the economic environment in general.

As for the sources, including paper texts, successful books and the internet, you are spoiled with choices.

The studying activity, however, never abandons the investor, even when he has become an expert. There is a pressing need not only to update continuously, but also to inquire about everything that gravitates around the securities in the portfolio.

7. Choose the long term

Investing in the stock market should not be an activity of a few months or even a few years. It must be a continuous activity. It is only through patience and perseverance that makes it possible to make substantial profits. This means that you need to build a long-term version, which might work at least for the next five years (even if ten are more suitable). This means that it is good not to give in to the temptation to sell the securities as soon as the prices start to fall. As the famous saying goes, "laugh well who laughs last."

8. Monitoring

If you opt for a long-term vision, as you should, then it is essential to monitor the status of your investment. Not everyone knows that control and monitoring begin before the investment itself. In particular, it is necessary to establish a benchmark (i.e. a yardstick) by means of which it is possible to really understand whether we are on the right path or not. Finally, it is good to make a periodic comparison between the expected results and the real ones. At the beginning, there is a strong temptation to abandon oneself to discouragement, also because the results tend to arrive later in time.

A general consideration can be made on the segment within which to operate. In fact, everything depends on risk tolerance. If this is very low, you should address those segments that by their nature do not suffer from the crisis. The reference is to those goods whose consumption is practically mandatory, like food and pharmaceutical products. Investing in pharmaceutical companies will not make you rich but it is a very useful asset to protect capital. Strangely enough, but up to a certain point, the high-tech segment (e.g. mobile phones, social networks, etc.) also play a similar role.

Investing in the stock market can be a business that can increase its capital. In addition to technical knowledge, we need some moral skills: patience, perseverance, lucidity, foresight. All qualities that must be cultivated and that can make the difference. The opposite will never give good fruits especially with an approach based on imprudence, on haste, from the frenzy of profit.

9. Use the leverage

What unfortunately many traders do not consider is investing in the stock market or trading online using leverage. To invest in the stock market with little money, it is necessary to deepen the study of this tool, which will allow us to expose our capital to a huge risk. We recommend the use of leverage only on a reduced capital, carried out concurrently also with a rationalized use of stop loss and take profit. In addition, you must always have your budget under control using careful Money Management. Finally, before investing in the stock market you need to study the markets and all the financial instruments on which you want to invest in.

10. You do not need to be a finance guru to invest in the stock market!

Obviously, we are not telling you that the market should not be studied or that there must be a basis for training. Someone who applies himself and follows the markets, deepening the subject, will always know more than others.

So, we always recommend following the training path of your broker, which will allow you not to make mistakes throughout the investment process. Taking advantage of the online trading demo platforms, it is possible to simulate the investment and understand where mistakes are made and avoid them when investing with a real account.

11. Use only trusty brokers

We believe that the stock market is not a market for everyone but for a chosen few! Above all, we cannot recommend the stock exchange. The investments on the stock exchange cannot be studied, even the basics and training. In this case, it is better to let go of one's own, as it is not possible to rely only on luck.

Our advice is to stay away if you do not have and do not want to learn specific skills. If you do not have a basic education, you will lose all the savings you invest in less than a month. On the contrary, instead, we recommend investing in the stock market with online trading and regulated brokers. This is because being regulated and being subjected to strict controls, they do not put capital at risk, and the broker will provide you with a fair and complete formation. Below you will find a complete list of regulated and authorized brokers to invest with.

12. Learn technical analysis

Technical analysis is the study of price trends with the use of graphs. The interest of a technical analyst is to look for the graphic configurations that are drawn by price movements. The market trend is evaluated to understand possible future price movements.

The pure technical analysis is not based on any fundament of the underlying activity, but it applies a series of technical tools drawn on the chart in order to allow for future courses.

On the chart, price movements are usually represented by bars or candles, allowing price analysis in a certain period called 'timeframe'.

On a candle, the body or the central part represents the difference between opening and closing in a given period. The shadows (i.e. the top and bottom segments) represent the difference between the maximum and the minimum of the period considered and the opening or closing of the candle.

We can have monthly, daily, 1 hour, 5 minutes or even shorter candles.

The different colours of the candles indicate a rise or fall in the period. Usually a green candle represents a rise in prices, which means that the closing price of the candle is higher than the opening one, while the red candle represents a drop.

The levels of the chart where prices find an obstacle are called 'levels of support or resistance'. A 'support' is the level at which a bearish price halts its downfall and potentially 'rebounds' up again. The most significant support is repeatedly tested and becomes the level of support from a technical point of view. The 'resistance' is the opposite of the support. It is the level at which a rising price finds an obstacle to rise further and instead shows a decline. Even a resistance tested several times takes on a higher strategic importance.

When prices determine an important level of support but then violate it downwards, this level of support becomes an important area of resistance. The same goes for a resistance that if violated on the upside, turns into a significant level of support.

There are so many indicators used by technical analysts to try to predict the next price movements. One of the most used indicators is the 'simple moving average', which is calculated on a certain amount of price data and is mobile because it moves from period to period.

Given an average of a certain period, the most recent data is added each time, eliminating the last data in the series from the calculation. The moving average can be used as a support or dynamic resistance. The most used periods on the daily chart for the moving average are 50, 100, and 200. If prices show an important uptrend, the moving average will be an important medium or short-term support; inversely if prices show a bearish trend, the average mobility will be a significant dynamic resistance.

13. Learn fundamental analysis

Unlike the previous one, it is based on the study of the company and its reference market.

In practice, it is based on balance sheet data, on management's ability and credibility, and on trends in the specific sector in which the company operates. In this case, one must also consider:

- value investing;

- growth investing; and

- investment.

All traders have a different investing style. Every trader has his own investment procedure and each has his own particular techniques, as well as his particular tricks and his particular "secrets."

However, do not be fooled by the strange idea of being able to learn how to invest by reading articles on the internet. This is impossible. You can find excellent advice but not the magic formula. At most, you could clear your mind and give yourself a general orientation, but to get serious you need longer and more in-depth things.

14. Analyse the state of the market

Closely connected to the concept of technical analysis and fundamental analysis is the concept of analysis of the general market. It does not matter whether you are a professional investor or a beginner, this will be the most difficult step you need to understand.

In practice, it is pure art applied to scientific instruments. You must first understand and analyse the market for the sole purpose of formulating a plausible development scenario. This also means accumulating an enormous amount of data and statistics regarding the performance of the securities and developing the "sensitivity" necessary to choose the truly relevant ones.

If you put this into practice, you will also understand why many investors buy the shares of a particular company.

At the same time, we always advise you to observe the products you have at home. Although this element may seem unusual, it is very important to understand that you have a direct knowledge of many products. In practice, it will allow you to perform a quick and intuitive analysis of the financial performance of the manufacturing companies, comparing them with those of their competitors.

Before investing you must reflect on the products examined. For example, try to imagine the economic conditions for which you might decide to stop buying them or increase or decrease your stocks. This is a great exercise to get a feeling of what an average person needs and treats as "important."

15. Create an investment plan

A very important step. You have to create an investment plan, but to do that you must first of all fully understand why you want to invest.

You must know how much you can invest and how much you want to invest to achieve your goals. You must also have clear ideas about what your goals are.

To do this you could always use an Excel sheet or even a special tool to calculate how much you will have to spend to achieve your goals.

Based on the income you can afford to invest, calculate the type of investment. You cannot claim to want to get $ 10,000 from an investment, if what you can afford to invest in trading online or on the stock exchange or even in other systems, do not exceed 1000 euros. Everything must be proportionate. Start small and build it up over time.

16. Understand Asset Location

Defined as the distribution of liquidity in the various investment instruments available should vary depending on the stage of life in which you are.

This means that if you are young, the percentage of your investment portfolio relative to the shares will have to be higher. On the contrary, if you have a solid and well-paid career, your job is like an obligation! You can use it in order to guarantee long-term income.

Here is how all this allows you to allocate most of your financial portfolio in shares.

At the same time, you have to understand that if you have a job whose remuneration is not predictable, as in the case where you are self-employed, then you have to allocate most of your financial portfolio in more stable products. In this case, it is better to invest in bonds, perhaps government bonds and not in shares.

At the same time, however, you must consider that the actions allow a faster growth of your invested assets but such situations entail a greater risk.

17. Study the financial risk

Another element to take into consideration when choosing to invest in a stock exchange is financial risk. We could define it as the risk linked to the fact that investment can go wrong.

This also assumes that the yield is lower than expected or may even go red.

So be careful not to underestimate this element. On the other hand, it is an element that is not easy to understand and accept. At the same time, it is not infrequent, and it is due to different dimensions that it is always good to know.

The financial risk has in fact different facets. In practice, it could be of different nature:

- Specific: linked to the performance of the single instrument we purchased;

- Systematic: linked to the oscillation of the financial market of the manager and linked to the skills of those who manage yours;

- Money related: be it an investment fund manager, or a financial planner, or consultant to whom you have been entrusted;

- Market timing: the possibility of making mistakes when entering and / or leaving the market;

- Liquidity: the possibility of having to sell a stock that has little market (it is called a little liquid title) and to have a low price; and lastly,

- Currency: when buying a security denominated in foreign currency, the yield will also depend on the ratio between the currency and the euro.

Analysed according to these elements, financial risk is a bit more complex than the simple possibility that things will go wrong. Understanding it and knowing how to manage these different risks can therefore shift the odds that things are going well in our favour.

18. Analyse and discover your risk tolerance

Another important element even before starting to invest in the stock market is to analyse one's risk appetite.

All financial instruments are characterized by a different risk. For example, the price of a stock varies over time more than that of a bond.

Unfortunately, this should not be considered as a reductive element. The risk is much higher than it might seem at first.

In fact, analysing a long-term time horizon and considering an investment in US stocks that have historically made very good progress and therefore considered as a safe investment, we must always consider the risk that we could incur the complete loss of capital invested for a joke of the market that you did not foresee. Therefore, you must also consider these factors.

Here, it is better to consider and analyse a more ambitious investment look. This means considering the investment portfolio and not the single instrument.

To date, there are different ways to make different instruments coexist; some of these are also quite risky. On the contrary, others can be considered less risky, and as such, reduces the overall risk of the investment.

19. Improve your Financial Intelligence

You are not born as a trader, but you can become one. Investors are not born like that, but they become one. How? By studying and applying. Here in this case, brokers offer you the right solution to your problem. Professional training courses, thanks to free video lessons such as those offered by the IQ Option broker, are dedicated entirely to the financial markets and online trading.

The financial competence takes into consideration two very important aspects: competence and time. These are very important elements that can really change the cards on the table and make a style of investment manageable and profitable that for others could become an anxiety-generating bloodbath.

Regarding the risk and its propensity to face it, the questions to be asked are 2.

- The first is inherent in the amount of time you can allocate to learn and therefore how much energy you are willing to devote to your investments; and

- The second is how anxious you are about money and economic security. In this case, it is better to let go of this whole investing idea.

20. Buy stocks of a company without competitors

Even this advice may seem improper, but in reality, it is very effective.

For example, it is never advisable to invest in retail and automotive airlines. Generally, they are not considered good long-term investments.

In most cases, these are commercial sectors in which competition is very high. This means that if you look at their balance sheets, you can see how the profits are very low.

In general, do not invest in companies that generate a large part of their turnover specifically when they have not shown profits and constant revenues even within a long period.

21. Keep yourself updated about the news in the market

Always try to find all possible information before buying any shares. Choose only companies that have a certain solidity. Choose those that have a price momentarily lower than their real value. This concept is the essence behind the investments. You buy low and sell high.

We consider it as the keystone of being disciplined in carrying out the researches, related market analyses, and in evaluating the performance of an investment by constantly checking it and making the necessary changes.

An example would be companies with an excellent brand, which can be a good investment option.

Coca-Cola, Johnson & Johnson, Procter & Gamble, 3M and Exxon are all good examples.

22. Do not look at your portfolio every hour

This is because markets are volatile. So, you do not have to be influenced by the performance of world stock exchanges, because otherwise you may even be tempted to liquidate your positions too early and you will lose an excellent long-term investment opportunity.

You must also consider before buying the shares of a stock, questions such as: If the value of my shares were to go down, would I be more inclined to liquidate or buy more?

If you decide to liquidate them, do not buy any other shares.

23. Be aware of your prejudices and do not allow the emotions to influence your decisions

You must always believe in what you do and never get overwhelmed by emotion. Always believe in yourself and in the strategy behind your investments. Only in this way, you will be on your way to become a successful investor.

All stock exchanges, like Wall Street, are focused on short-term investments.

This is why it is difficult to predict possible future profits, in case they are projected in the long term.

In order to calculate the target of your investment (the price at which to sell your positions), make forecasts with a time horizon of more than 10 years and update them over time using the DCF.

24. Invest in those companies that hold shareholders in high esteem

In most cases, companies prefer to spend profits on buying a new personal jet for the CEO instead of paying dividends to shareholders.

A long-term management-oriented remuneration system, "stock-expensing", even if it is a prudent capital investment policy, a reliable dividend policy, a profit for growth stocks and the BVPS ("Book-Value-Per- Share ") are all indicators of a company oriented towards its shareholders.

25. Try out "paper trading"

In this case, it is a simulation of investments. In practice, this tool keeps track of the price of the shares and of all of your purchase and sale transactions, as if you were actually operating them on the market.

At the same time, you can check your investments if they have generated a profit or not.

Once you have identified a reliable and profitable strategy and you feel comfortable with the natural functioning of the market, you can move on to the real operational phase.

Finally, remember that you are not buying and selling worthless pieces of paper; the price rises and falls over time; you are buying shares in real companies.

Your decision to buy the shares of a particular company should be influenced only by two factors: the economic soundness of the company and the price of its shares.

26. Focus your thoughts

When analysing the market, you should always try to formulate a plausible development scenario and consequently identify the good securities to invest in. We are sure that this passage serves by providing some forecasts on some specific areas.

An example would be the trend in interest rates and inflation, if not the way in which these variables can affect the yield of fixed-rate financial products or other assets. At the same time, when interest rates are low, it could be expected that consumers and businesses can access cash and credit more easily.

In practice, all this means that people have more money to use for their purchases and therefore tend to buy more.

At the same time, companies, thanks to higher revenues, will be able to invest with the aim of expanding their activities.

On the contrary, the opposite happens in the stock market; low interest rates lead to an increase in the price of equities. At the same time, a high interest rate generates a decrease in the value of the shares.

At a time when interest rates are high, investing becomes much more expensive. So, you could try to invest in shares that offer a better return for you but are not that heavy for consumers.

A good example could be a bank's shares. If you invest on the shares of a Bank X because the interest rates are high for you, you must also consider the interest rates that are applied to those who ask for a mortgage, for example. In this case, an interest rate for a high mute will soon make Bank shares collapse because it is not convenient for the lender. Always evaluate all factors then.

In short, consumers spend less and companies have less liquidity for investments and therefore there is a slowdown in economic growth or even a stalemate.

27. Create a wish list

In order to be able to establish your financial goals, you must always have a precise idea of the things or experiences you wish to possess. You can always choose only what you want to experience in life, and for which you need to earn money.

You must have a list of everything you want to get from this investment and then work out a line-up to guarantee your goals.

28. Diversify your portfolio

Investors with experience like Warren Buffett recommend diversifying their investments. A choice that serves to manage risks in a better way, as do the most prudent that focus on companies in different industries and in different countries, hoping that a bad event does not damage all their titles: "Imagine owning five different companies. At the end of the year the company A and B performed well and increased the value of the shares by 25%. C and D instead increased by 10%. While E was the unlucky and ended up in liquidation. In this case the diversification strategy helps you recover the losses of your total investment.

29. Understand the main financial instruments

Among the many solutions that are available to those who intend to invest, we want to talk about: Forex, binary options, ETFs, and commodities.

Proceeding by order, we clarify how Forex investments work. It is the largest market in the world today. Although it is simple to deposit and therefore invest in the ratio of currencies, it is certainly known that returns are so high as the same measure of losses. It is for this reason that experts are always advised to take advantage of the demos for general learning before proceeding with the use of real money. In any case, it is our advice to beginners to focus only on the performance of a currency pair, remembering to include the stop loss in the open position to avoid too large losses.

Regarding investments in binary options, these are available to anyone, like the previous solution, provided that some attention is always paid in these circumstances. This investment system concerns the launch of forecasts aimed at the performance of a certain security over a given period of time. It is expected that the course will sometimes be positive or negative and it will depend on the trader who can go from a minimum of 60 seconds up to months. If the forecast is correct, there will be rather interesting profits. Even here, in order not to face unpleasant surprises, the same goes for the previous type of investment.

The ETF, those funds listed in real time that we mentioned, which go to replicate the index of a certain basket of securities, allow you to invest even with small amounts at lower costs than traditional funds. With these you can trade on a wide variety of indices such as emerging markets, entire geographical areas, individual states, listed companies and more. The advantages of investing using ETFs reside not only in their convenience, in being very liquid and tradable like equities, but also in the respective assets independent of the issuer.

30. Consider it a serious business

I believe that anyone can learn to trade options, currencies (Forex), commodities or cryptocurrencies. In the same way, I am convinced that with this system you can become financially free.

But it must be approached as a serious business.

Let me ask you a question: how much did you study or work to achieve the experience you have in your current job? I imagine we are talking about several years and still thousands of hours of study and practice.

Trading is not different. When trading, you compete against a lot of people who do it by profession; you must therefore have humility, work, perseverance, intelligence and method. If you really apply, in a few months you can decide to give up your job because you can earn a lot of money with something that requires commitment and constancy, but without being stressed or having to spend all day on the trading sites.

Chapter 2:
Three ways to jump start your investing experience

Are you looking for safe and profitable investments? Finding solutions of this type is not easy, you know that very well and that's why you decided to take the smartphone, the PC or the tablet to deepen.

In this chapter we have decided to provide you with 3 concrete solutions to invest immediately, without making endless queues at the bank and without losing control of what you do.

The strategies that we suggest are ordered according to the risk profile, so we start from the less risky ones then get to the more aggressive ones later.

We have written it in several books of this series, we underline it here too for safety: there are no safe investments and at the same time with double-digit returns. The times of government bonds and generous postal coupons have long since come to a close, the current economic situation sees interest at historic lows owing to the ECB's manoeuvres in recent years.

In summary:

> *Few risks = Few Earnings*
>
> *Many Risks = Potentially Increased Earnings but High Chances of Huge Losses*

We come now to the merit of our discussion; here are the best solutions for investing that we have chosen for you.

1. Santander Consumer Bank is the most remunerative deposit account

Are you looking for 100% capital guarantee? The deposit account is the best solution even if, in light of the considerations made before, you do not have to expect double-digit returns.

The best deposit account of the moment is that of Santander Consumer Bank which offers you an annual 1.8% on deposits at 36 months.

The advantages of Santander's offer can be summarized as follows:

- 100% security;

- Open it online: no stress, if you are from a PC you just need to fill out a form (you can do the same thing if you are on a smartphone) and just leave a little data. The procedure will be completed by phone at the time you indicated;

- No penalty in case of early release: if you withdraw money before the scheduled time, you lose nothing; and

- Opening costs and management fees: you do not have to pay anything to make money.

To all this, we must add that Santander also provides the unconstrained option that allows you to receive 0.5% per year on free sums. This option can be mixed with the tied one: for example, out of 30 thousand euros, 20 thousand can be tied up at an interest rate of 1.8%, while the remaining 10 thousand free ones receive 0.5%.

Santander is a solid institution, active throughout the world with 122 million customers and over 160 years of history and is now the best solution for those looking for a deposit account free of risks and concerns.

2. MoneyFarm: the tech alternative to deposit accounts

Moneyfarm is an American startup that has created a convenient platform to invest online: it is safe and easy to understand, we have also explained it in our review.

You can earn up to 5.41%.

The bank deposit accounts, at this stage, have returns that only in a few cases exceed 1.5%. If you're looking for granitic safety, go back to paragraph 1 where we talk about Santander.

However, if you are looking for better profitability at the same risk, you should pay attention to what you are reading. MoneyFarm, in fact, is an alternative to deposit accounts because it offers balanced investments with an almost similar degree of risk.

By signing up for MoneyFarm you have the following advantages:

- Personal assistance of a team of competent advisors;
- Choose where to invest by filling in the questionnaire in which you indicate your degree of risk;

- You can start testing the goodness of the platform even with a small capital: just $ 500 is enough to try.

With MoneyFarm you can plan your investments and earn up to 5.41% per year, choosing the composition of your portfolio based on your risk profile.

Moneyfarm aims to invest in funds with lower operating costs and to guarantee maximum transparency to customers.

You can start investing immediately, even with $ 500. Before choosing the strategy, the team of experts helps you to plan your goals exactly.

Registration is free: it takes 3 minutes to start to know it, you can also try it on a smartphone as it is really very easy to use.

Unlike many structured platforms for high risk investments (think of trading or options), Moneyfarm allows you to operate even if you have a low risk appetite and is undoubtedly a real alternative to deposit accounts or other banking products that make a lot less.

The portfolios are constantly monitored by team of experts and free assistance is guaranteed for the entire duration of the relationship.

It is possible to use the live chat service or to set up a telephone appointment thanks to a special toll-free number. The seriousness is certified by the prizes and awards obtained by leading international financial experts and opinions on the web that are definitely positive. You also choose how much you are willing to risk, and the staff helps you plan the route step by step.

3. Social Trading

Compared to the previous solution, we are facing a decidedly riskier way: let's underline it immediately, to avoid misunderstandings. If the world of finance interests you, keep reading carefully because you found what you were looking for.

Have you ever tried to approach online trading? If you did and you gave up, most likely you came across the difficulties of a world where only the professional traders, that is, have experience, years of study and time to constantly monitor what is happening in the market in which they operate.

The social trading we want to talk about is created to solve this gap in skills between professional and non-professional investors. eToro, the first social trading platform, allows you to make copy trading: you can, in other words, copy the winning strategies of top traders emulating their successes.

The principle is simple: by investing as the best, you earn like the best.

How does eToro work?

eToro allows its members to copy the strategies of the best American and world traders, called popular investors. Top traders are certified and chosen among the best that invest through the platform.

In particular, you can order them and select the ones that interest you the most according to two criteria:

Earnings - Simple: see who made the most money in a given period of time (6 months, 12 months, 24 months) and copy from those who have achieved gains of 25%;

Risks - If you want to adopt a more conservative strategy, you only need to copy from traders who say they risk less, so as to limit your exposure to losses.

With eToro it is possible to invest in the following markets:

- stocks;
- forex;

- cryptocurrency;

- commodities; an

- CFD.

Of course, copying from the best does not completely eliminate the risks because past earnings are not a guarantee for the future. You will agree, however, that when you decide to dedicate yourself to finance risk is part of the game and with social trading you have the opportunity to take it down in the initial phase and learn from the best.

There are already 4.5 million investors who have relied on social trading to invest like the best: if finance fascinates you and you do not think you have a great experience, eToro is the most effective solution to start investing.

To start, you only need to:

- Create an eToro account;

- Choose the trader to copy from, taking care to select one with a strategy similar to your goals;

- Deciding how much to invest: $ 190 is enough to start copying from the best ones.

eToro is a win-win system designed to share knowledge and earnings and is the best way to debut on the stock market.

Chapter 3:
What is the stock market?

Everyone or almost everyone has already heard of the stock exchange or its most popular assets, such as the MIB 30 and other indexes or shares of major global companies.

But few among the non-professionals really know the meaning of these technical terms and that they are (wrongly) considered reserved for the most aggressive traders.

In fact, the Exchange is a market accessible to everyone, whether through banking products, such as securities accounts or accumulation plans, or through an online trading platform.

A brief description of the stock market

Contrary to what one might think, the history of the stock exchange is quite old, even though its concept has largely evolved over time. Indeed, the stock exchange made its appearance in the fourteenth century in Brussels, Belgium.

Today, even if the stock market is always a place of exchange, it is first and foremost an immense market in which financial securities are exchanged. These financial securities may relate to the shares of large companies, bonds, currencies or even commodities such as gold or oil.

However, in this case it is not a matter of exchanging physical products or merchandise, but only of securities that represent a certain evolutionary value.

General operation of the stock market

Stocks could therefore be defined as a market in which buyers and sellers meet. But, unlike the traditional market, it is not the sellers who decide the price of their securities but the buyers.

It is then the order book that accounts for the prices decided in this way.

Ultimately, the more the securities of a stock market are required by the buyers, the higher the price goes up. On the contrary, when demand is weaker, their prices fall.

The stock market on which securities can be traded is also called the "primary market". It is therefore on this market that companies can issue what are called "shares", that are then bought by investors, private individuals or professionals.

Thanks to these purchases of securities, companies can obtain the money necessary to make investments.

But the shares are not the only assets traded on this market since there can also be bonds or financial securities.

Investors' interest is speculative given that they buy a security at a price considered lower than the price that could subsequently reach for a gain or receive what are called "dividends" according to the economic performance of the issuing company of these securities becoming " shareholders ".

A market with international reach

Thanks to this system of securities and the advent of new technologies, the stock market has strongly developed on an international scale. Today there are almost as many stock exchanges as there are capitalist countries, although in most cases this market is virtual and does not include physical "trading rooms", the latter replaced by complex computer networks.

To better understand the importance of the stock exchange, know that in the single financial centre of Milan, billions of euros are exchanged every day.

Trading times on the stock exchange

Maybe you do not know it but trading on the stock exchange offers the possibility of dealing online continuously or 24 hours a day, thanks to the overlapping of the opening hours of the different international stock markets. In fact, the world's big financial centres are eight and their trading hours are listed in three major sessions: the Asian session, the European session and the North American session.

But we must also take into account the legal and solar hours that are not the same depending on the time zone. Let's take a look at the most influential time zones for the stock market.

The Asian session

At the beginning of the week the Asian session is the first one to open. This session includes the stock exchange centres of Japan, China, Australia, New Zealand and Russia as well as other smaller centres. Asian assets and currency pairs including currencies of these countries are therefore the most volatile in these times. The same applies to economic publications.

The trading hours of the Asian session are as follows:

Opening hours of the Asian market: at 4 in summer and 3 in winter

Closing time of the Asian market: at 8 in summer and 7 in winter

The European session:

The European session is obviously the most interesting for European investors. It is the second to open after the Asian session and also regroups several major stock exchanges including Italy, France, Germany, Switzerland or the United Kingdom. It should be noted that London's financial centre is the largest in the world and more than 30% of financial transactions are carried out in this centre every day. Trading volumes are therefore very high during the European session and therefore involve extremely volatile and interesting movements in terms of trading.

The trading hours of the European session are as follows:

European market opening hours: 12.00 in the summer and 12.00 in the winter

Closing time of the European market: at 16 in summer and at 17 in winter

The North American session:

Finally comes the North American session, which is therefore the last to open and close the market cycle. Obviously, this session is also one of the most followed by traders all over the world because it is during this period that US assets are traded. This session includes the financial markets of the United States but also of Canada, Mexico and the countries of South America. It is on the stock market in New York that the volatility is higher at this time of day.

The trading hours of the North American session are as follows:

Opening time of the North American market: at 17 in summer and at 17 in winter

Closing time of the North American market: at 21 in summer and at 22 in winter

History and general knowledge

The Stock Exchange is the market where sellers and buyers can trade values, foreign currencies, services and goods. The stock exchange thus becomes an important place to put companies in touch, looking for resources to support their production, and investors.

Already in the Middle Ages, the scholarship gathered merchants and notaries who dedicated themselves to mercantile and financial activities.

In the twelfth century, Venice became the main Italian square; here were introduced some innovations later adopted by other cities such as the negotiation of the public debt and the turn of the bill.

Bruges, in West Flanders, is the first European city to have a physical place for exchange, where the sale takes place according to new stock exchange rules. The industrial revolution leads to the birth of the modern stock exchange in Italy, following the example of Bruges (Trieste, Rome, Milan, Florence, Naples, Turin, Genoa, Bologna, Palermo and Venice).

We can distinguish two types of market based on the services and products exchanged:

- the stock exchange;
- the commodities exchange.

The Stock Exchange is the market in which financial instruments already in circulation are exchanged, such as bonds, shares, futures, warrants, etc.; as a consequence, the stock exchange is a secondary market (in the primary markets, investors buy the goods as soon as they reach the market).

In the commodities exchange, the sale involves goods of different types, placed in appropriate warehouses. Here buyers and sellers can exchange the deposit policies, which guarantee the presence of the goods and the right of withdrawal.

The sale and purchase of outstanding securities is regulated by precise rules; once the system of the on-call auction was over, where the agents exchanged paper documents, the market takes place via an electronic circuit where it is also possible to exchange government bonds and bonds.

Among the main types of shares we distinguish the ordinary ones, as they assign precise administrative and financial rights to the holder (right to vote in the meetings, to request assembly, liquidation, option, etc.).

Preferred stock (preferred shares) guarantee special property rights to the owners; in the event of dissolution of the company, for example, "privileges" are granted in the distribution of profits (as provided for in the company by-laws).

Savings shares grant ownership rights to assets; however, they exclude administrative rights, including the right to vote.

Poster-gate shares provide for limitations in both administrative and patrimonial rights (generally excluding voting rights).

Limited-voting shares include special restrictions on administrative rights, such as voting limited to certain topics; according to the American law, they must guarantee property privileges to the owner.

As previously mentioned, the financial market is structured in financial centres, where various financial services are treated.

The largest financial centre is New York, where the NYSE is located (the New York Stock Exchange of all commodities), the Nasdaq (technology stocks) and the AmEx (the American Stock Exchange collects many small capitalization companies that sell securities of various kinds).

Other important financial centres include Tokyo and London (the most important in Europe).

Different types of investment

Now that we have understood what the stock market is, let's dive into three other ways to invest your money before moving on. There are 3 types of possibilities that we want to discuss. In particular, these are option trading, forex trading and day trading.

Option trading

Options are a great financial instrument that allows common investors to get a greater revenue out of their investment. With option trading, you have the possibility to bet against or in favour of a stock and make money both on the way up and on the way down. The capital exposed is minimal and the returns can be great. It takes a bit more work than just buying a stock and holding it, but it is also a path that can be followed.

Forex trading

When people think about trading, they mostly think about the forex market. Forex trading allows people to speculate on the variations of value of the different currencies. This is the biggest market available and counts millions of traders. It is something that should be done only by professionals or very experienced traders, since 99% of people that invest in forex lose money over time. If you want to try it out, do it at your own risk and wit a little portion of your portfolio.

Day trading

When you invest in a stock usually you think about holding it for a few months or even a few years. With day trading, instead, the action is much faster and everything happens quickly. With day trading you are operating on the stock market or the forex market but you are doing a lot of operations every day (this is where the name comes from). Of course, by day trading you are risking much more than with a common "buy and hold" approach, but the return can be greater.

Chapter 4:

What is an IPO?

A good definition of IPO is that the Initial Public Offering, an instrument governed by the law through which a company obtains the dissemination of its titles among the public. Using what is technically called the creation of the float, the company obtains the listing of its securities on the regulated market.

Some of these terms may seem difficult. For those who are just beginners we can say that the IPO is a solicitation to invest. Thus, the Initial Public Offering is a real invitation to invest. Having clarified the meaning of IPO let's move on.

How does the Initial Public Offer work? The legislative background of this application is represented by the Consolidated Law on Finance (Legislative Decree 58/1998). This law provides for a whole series of provisions on information and transparency. The indistinct public of the subjects potentially interested in the IPO (recipients of the offer) has the right to know all the useful information to decide whether to join the IPO in full awareness.

The IPO process is decidedly long and complex. By regulation, the IPO foresees the involvement of a series of very different subjects. The following subjects participate in the various phases of the Initial Public Offering:

- the issuing company;
- the global coordinator;
- the sponsor;
- the specialist;
- the financial advisor;
- the law firms in charge; and
- the members of the placement consortium.

When one wonders how the IPO works, it should be noted that the first phase of the process is represented by the sending to SEC of the prior communication from the company concerned. The prior communication is an official document that the company presents to the SEC. The same company that aims to be listed on the stock exchange is responsible for drawing up the Prospectus according to the legal framework.

From what we have said, it is easy to deduce that an IPO can last even a month. If you then consider the whole procedure for admission to the stock market then you also get to 4 or even 6 months. In short, before betting on the performance of what's listed, one must allow quite a bit of time to pass. This prolonging, of course, also has an impact on the possibility of trading on the shares of that listed company.

Book building an IPO

When referring to this method for fixing the price of the offer on the stock exchange, the first question concerns the definition of book building. With this strange term, we indicate the process by which the application form of the institutional investors who have submitted an order concerning a security offer transaction is drafted. Through this process the price of the same securities is set.

The IPO book building provides for the formation of the price range through the demand expressed by the institutional investors themselves.

The global coordinator manages this process. This figure has the task of collecting all the purchase / subscription orders of institutional investors in a book called the institutional book. Orders are collected based on price or time priority or size. Each order can be expressed in number of shares or in counter value. Finally, each order is linked to the price limit indicated by the originator.

Through this process it is possible to draw a curve which shows the price of the IPO.

Chapter 5:
What are mutual funds and how to use them

Mutual funds are financial institutes whose purpose is to invest the funds raised by savers. The aim is to create value, through the management of a series of assets, for the fund managers and for the investors who have invested in it.

There are three main components that characterise a mutual fund (later simply fund):

- The fund's participants are the investors who invest in the fund's assets, acquiring shares through their capital;

- The management company, which is the management hub of the fund's activities, which has the function of starting the fund itself, of establishing its own regulation and managing its portfolio; and

- Depositary banks which physically hold the fund's securities and keep cash in hand. The banks also have a controlling role on the legitimacy of the fund's assets on the basis of the provisions of the Bank of America and the fund regulations.

The costs incurred by those who enter into a mutual fund are the following:

- The entry or subscription commission paid at the time of the first payment. It is generally inversely proportional to the size of its investment (the more you invest, the less you pay) and it is higher for the so-called equity funds than for the balanced ones. There are also funds that do not provide for an entry fee: they are the so-called no-load funds

- The management fee, on the other hand, is the cost borne by the cross-party fund manager. It is calculated on an annual basis, but generally paid on a six-monthly, quarterly or monthly basis.

- The extra-commission of performance is instead an optional commission that some self-financing funds in order to reward if, thanks to their ability, the fund's return exceeds a certain threshold based on pre-established parameters

The unit value of each individual share of the various funds is published daily in the newspapers. On the NASDAQ website it is also possible to follow the price trend of the shares of the various funds in exactly the same way that the trend of the shares is followed. The prices in question already incorporate the return on the fund.

There are various types of mutual funds, the best known are the following three:

- Equity funds invest mainly in shares or convertible bonds. They are generally riskier but tend to guarantee higher returns and in any case guarantee lower fluctuations than simple equity securities as they generally balance their share with non-equity investments such as ordinary bonds, government securities and with the liquidity held. Another way in which risk balancing is generally achieved is to differentiate by geographical area and therefore also by evaluating the fund's investments;

- Bond funds, these are funds that invest mainly in ordinary bonds and government bonds: this type of funds generally has the advantage of being less risky, but the disadvantage of being less profitable; and

- Balanced funds are funds that aim to balance the various forms of investment in order to obtain performance and risk profiles initiated between those of equity and bond funds.

Chapter 6:
Where to buy and sell stocks

The use of shares, whether it is to collect dividends or to speculate on their listing, is an increasingly widespread and interesting practice. The risk of loss is always present but depending on the way you buy and sell your shares, this risk can be reduced. If you are wondering how to buy and sell the shares of large listed companies online, here are some explanations that may interest you.

Buy shares to become shareholders

A large part of private individuals and institutions that buy Stocks do so in order to become shareholders.

It is the simplest use of actions and their main purpose.

In fact, when a company issues its shares, it is possible to buy them directly online.

However, for the already listed shares, to do so it is necessary to go through an intermediary, which can be an online broker or an online bank.

Of course, it is also possible to buy shares directly from sellers who have bought these shares previously, as well as re-sell your shares.

Buy and sell shares with online banks

The easiest way to buy and sell shares is to go through one of the placement products offered by banks and, in particular, by online banks. Thanks to 100% online operation of these banks, you can easily pass your purchase and sale orders directly via the internet without moving.

The advantages of this system are numerous because it is your bank that will take care of executing your orders and then buying and selling your shares. To take advantage of stock market shares through these systems, you must underwrite an Investment Plan in Shares, a securities account or a life insurance, which are the main banking products on the stock market.

The only drawback of this method concerns the expenses that may be higher than those that you would have to pay if you bought and sold the shares yourself.

However, bank commissions rarely exceed 4%.

One of the main advantages of bank placement products is that your purchases and sales of shares are supervised by market intermediaries and you can benefit from advice.

Buy and sell shares with online brokers

Another method is to contact an online mediator. Their operation is almost identical to that of online banks, with the difference that you do not enjoy assistance and advice, but at the same time the costs are lower because you decide for yourself what actions to buy or sell.

These online brokers also allow trading through stock market shares without actually having to buy them. To do this, you just need to speculate on the evolution of their value. The tools that allow you to proceed in this way are CFDs.

Ultimately there are several methods to buy and sell shares on the internet. Before deciding on one or the other of these solutions, take care to correctly evaluate the commissions involved as well as your level of knowledge on the stock exchange. Depending on these criteria, each of these two methods has different advantages. It is also good to understand the quotation system of an action to be able to speculate on this type of assets.

How much does the purchase or sale of the shares cost?

To answer this question, it is essential to define the strategy that will be adopted to buy or sell your shares.

If you own a stock portfolio through the intermediation of a stock market product, each investment in the purchase or sale will have a cost corresponding to the expenses called "brokerage expenses". These expenses can take various forms and involve different costs depending on the share traded (national, European or international market), the amount of the transaction carried out and, obviously, the intermediary. They can be in the form of a fixed or percentage cost on the amount of the transaction. It is therefore very important to carefully choose your stock market offer and your partner by consulting in advance the details of the charges applied to stock market orders.

Things are simpler for online trading and expenses are generally lower. In fact, to be sure, there are no defined brokerage fees for the sale or purchase of shares on the Stock Exchange from a trading platform through CFDs. Obviously, the mediator has a remuneration, however, but in a different and more transparent form: he applies the spread.

The spread corresponds to a small difference between the real quotation of an asset and the quotation of purchase or sale. As a result, when buying shares, the purchase price will be slightly higher than the real price of the asset in question and, in the case of a sale of shares, the selling price will be slightly lower than the real asset price.

Also, in this case, the spreads can vary from one broker to another and, depending on the type of shares you intend to sell or buy, it is interesting to compare the different spreads applied before opening your online account. The spreads can also be fixed and do not vary or be variable and evolve according to the market situation.

What shares can be bought or sold online?

For some years now, the offer of mediators in terms of CFDs on shares has been considerably enriched and it is now possible to access many stocks from the trading platforms made available to the general public.

Of course, you will find European and international stocks. All the stocks proposed by these platforms are part of the large international stock indexes and are therefore particularly popular and volatile and offer many possibilities thanks to a precise strategy based on technical and fundamental data.

Chapter 7:
Is it worth it to invest in stocks?

In this historical moment the search for high returns has become almost spasmodic. Unfortunately, the expansionary policy of central banks has caused the collapse of yields (now virtually 0). Anyone who wants to get a positive return must take risks.

In this context, many are deciding to invest in stocks. What we will be tackling in this chapter is whether it is really worth investing in stocks. The answer? It certainly is worth it, but it all depends on the modality of the investment.

This is an investment that can still guarantee very high performance, provided, however, if one's to follow some guidelines.

The first tip is to use only really affordable platforms to invest in stocks. Among the best we can definitely remember Plus500 or Markets. These platforms are characterized by the fact that they are very easy to use, even for those who have never worked with the actions but, at the same time, guarantee advanced tools, suitable even for the most experienced and needs. At the time of registration, you will receive a free bonus that amounts to 7,000 euros for Plus500 and 4,000 euros for Markets. This is additional capital that can be used to operate on the stock markets but cannot be directly withdrawn. If you use the bonus and you get profits, these profits can instead be taken without any problems or constraints.

Both Plus500 and Markets are Trading Contracts for Difference (CFD) trading platforms: this is a particularly flexible and easy-to-understand derivative instrument that guarantees the possibility of obtaining high profits both when markets rise, and markets fall. This is the second condition that makes it worthwhile to invest in stocks: if you buy shares directly you earn only when the markets go up. And in today's financial conditions, it's an immense gamble. At this time, it is absolutely not convenient to buy shares, the thing that must be done is to subscribe derivatives (such as CFDs that are very simple) that have underlying actions. Plus500 and Markets are the ideal solution for investing in stocks and, incidentally, they also allow investing in forex, indices, commodities, bitcoins, etc.

If you want to invest in shares and you want to earn money, the advice is to open an account on Markets or on Plus500.

The big advantage of stock investing: leverage

Through the use of financial leverage (or simply "leverage") a person has the possibility to buy or sell financial assets for an amount higher than the capital held and, consequently, to benefit from a higher potential return than that deriving from a direct investment in the underlying and, conversely, to expose yourself to the risk of very significant losses.

Let's see how the concept of leverage works starting from a simple case. Let's assume you have $ 100 available to invest Leverage financial in a stock. Let's assume that the gain or loss expectations are equal to 30%: if things go well, we will have $ 130, otherwise, we will have $ 70. This is a simple speculation in which we bet on a particular event.

In case we decide to risk more investing, in addition to our $ 100, also another $ 900 borrowed, then the investment would take a different articulation because we use a leverage of 10 to 1 (we invest $ 1000 having a capital initial only of 100). If things go well and the stock goes up 30%, we will receive $ 1300, we return the 900 borrowed with a gain of $ 300 on an initial capital of 100. So, we get a 300% profit with a stock that gave a 30 in return. Obviously on the $ 900 borrowed we will have to pay an interest, but the general principle remains valid: the leverage allows one to increase the possible gains.

Considering the further case of the investment in derivatives; let's assume we buy a derivative that, within a month, gives the right to buy 100 grams of gold at a price set today at $ 5,000. We could physically buy the gold with an outlay of 5000 $ and keep it waiting for the price to rise and then sell it back. If we decide instead to use derivatives, we should not have $ 5,000, but only the capital needed to buy the derivative. Let's say that a bank sells for 100 $ the derivative that allows us to buy the same 100 grams of gold in a month to $ 5,000. If in a month the gold is worth 5,500, we can buy it and sell it immediately, realizing a gain of 500 $. With the 100 $ of the price of the derivative, we make a profit of $ 400, or 400%, with $ 100.

Without using derivatives and leverage, the same $500 I could have earned them only against an investment of $ 5,000, making a profit of 10%.

What are the potentials of its use?

The potential of leveraging is clear. But be careful: the leverage multiplier effect, described with the previous examples, works even if the investment goes wrong. For example, if we decide to invest $ 100 in our possession plus an additional sum of $ 900 borrowed, if the stock depreciated by 30%, we would remain with only $ 700 in hand; having to return the $ 900 borrowed plus interest and considering the $ 100 of our initial investment we would have a loss of over $ 300 on an initial capital of $ 100. As a percentage, the loss would therefore be 300% against a reduction in the value of the share of 30%.

Another element to keep in mind is that the different financial levers can be combined: in this way speculation operations are carried out using a "squared lever" with clear reflections on potential aptitudes.

What may appear to be an interesting tool with positive potential for the investor, on the other hand, presents risks that must therefore be taken into due consideration. In fact, if the financial system as a whole works with a very high leverage and financial institutions lend money to each other to multiply the possible profits, the loss of an individual investor can trigger a domino effect by infecting the entire financial market.

Banks are typically entities that operate with a more or less high degree of leverage: against a certain net capital, the total assets in which the resources are invested are generally much higher. For example, a bank with equity of $ 100 and leverage of 20 manages assets for $ 2,000. A loss of 1% of the assets entails the loss of 20% of the equity capital.

The development of the market for the transfer of credit risk (from financial intermediaries to the market) has meant that the traditional bank model, called "originate-and-hold" ("create and hold": the bank that provided the loan remains in the balance sheet until maturity), has been substituted for many operators from the "originated-to-distribute" ("create and distribute": the intermediary selects the debtors, but then transfers the loan to others, recovering the liquidity and the regulatory capital previously committed or the pure credit risk (credit derivatives), with benefits only on capital requirements), with the effect of a further increase in leverage. The spread of this second bank model is one of the factors that explain the crisis triggered on the sub-prime mortgage market.

Property price inflation has supported the issuance of securitized loans and the exponential growth of the related market, allowing banks to make huge profits and, at the same time, increase leverage. But "the money machine" could not last long and in the end many banks found themselves without sufficient capital to absorb the losses deriving from the inversion of the real estate market trend, resulting in fact as failed companies.

In the meantime, the example of the banks has spread within the financial system by spreading to all other financial institutions: leverage had prevailed, especially in the United States, generating a huge volume of risky investments that rested on a fraction infinitesimal of equity capital. We are thinking of the issue of so-called "credit default swaps" (derivative instruments used to hedge against the default risk of the debtor): some insurance companies were heavily exposed to the real estate market and when the latter collapsed and the value of mortgages fell, they began to lose without having sufficient capital to absorb the losses deriving from the issue of those instruments.

In order not to risk failing and return to sufficient levels of bank capital, capital increases can be used (not an easy task in times of crisis), the reduction of the amount of loans to businesses (granting fewer new loans and not renewal of those already issued) and the disposal of other liquid assets (mostly shares). The result of all this, in the period of the sub-prime crisis, was a credit freeze and a collapse of the stock market. These are the main channels through which the financial crisis has hit the real economy. Credit rationing affected investments and the fall in the stock market (which adds to the decline in house prices) has reduced the value of household wealth and therefore consumption.

We know that a certain level of leverage is physiological to sustain economic growth, even if we have no indication of what the optimal level is. But history teaches us how in an increasingly globalized and interdependent economic-financial system, leverage can be a trigger for speculative bubbles. And it is in these periods that the strongest disconnection between finance and the real economy is generated.

Earning potential

The stock market gives the false impression that making money on the stock market is just a matter of choosing the right securities, investing quickly, staying glued to a computer screen and spending the day obsessing over what the investment is.

But the truth about how to make money on the stock market is another and you'll find out by reading the following pages.

The secret that reveals how to earn on the Stock Exchange, buying or selling securities and shares, is well explained by the thought of an investor known throughout the world, Benjamin Graham:

"Real money is made not by buying and selling, but by owning the securities, receiving interest and dividends and taking advantage of the increase in their value in the long term".

In a simpler way, the first secret to understanding how to earn on the stock market according to Graham is to focus on long-term investments, keeping a stock for at least 5 years in your investment portfolio.

Including the first fundamental concept of investing in the stock market, we now analyse concretely how to earn by buying stocks.

Investing in the stock market, buying and selling stocks, for many people is a very attractive prospect. However, we are talking about a real investment, accompanied by risk, and it is necessary to understand that it is not easy to earn on the stock market as some may want to make you believe.

To understand how to do this, we need to be aware of what we are doing and what the factors that influence the success or failure are of our investment.

Many prefer to turn to a financial advisor and leave it to him to follow the market trend; others more enterprising opt for the choice to invest through CFD or to buy shares through an intermediary.

On the stock exchange you earn and lose, and the certainty of the result is not always quantifiable.

That's why it is essential to know what the mechanisms of gains and losses are on the stock market, and therefore how to earn on the stock market, as well as knowing how the stock market works.

Investing in the stock market, buying or selling shares, involves investing in one or more of the many companies listed on the stock exchange, both in America and abroad.

Companies have an interest in listing on the Stock Exchange to find new financial resources necessary for their production processes.

The investor does not invest for the glory or to favour one company over another, but to have a profit and to earn with the difference between the purchase price and the selling price.

But how can one make money with stock market shares? Every little saver can decide to invest part of his savings in shares, that is, fractions of corporate capital traded on the stock exchange.

Assume that today in some shares have a nominal value of 11.00 euros and a market value of 12.50 euros thanks to an appreciation of the stock following a statement by the company's ad on a contract in the North Europe.

The investor wants to earn on the stock exchange and decides to buy 10,000 of those shares through an intermediary. The cost of investing in the stock market will be the number of shares for the price per share. In our case it is 125.000 euro (12.50 * 10.000), to which must be added commission costs for the operation, which vary from intermediary to intermediary.

The following week, the same shares recorded a rise following the positive result of the quarterly report. The price of those share rises to 13.80, a price higher than that to which the investor has paid the shares (12.50).

The investor decides to sell the 10,000 shares bought the previous week. The broker will give the investor the current value of the shares. This will then have to return 138,000 euros (13.80 * 10,000), then withholding the amount of the commission.

And here, one is explained how to earn on the stock market.

The realized gain is obtained with the difference between the sale value (or € 138,000 - commissions) and the purchase cost of the securities (ie € 125,000 +

commissions): in our example we have a profit of € 12,750.00 (137,850- 125,100).

But if the price of the shares fell, however, from 12.50 to 10.00 euros and the investor had decided to sell, then the result would be a loss.

Chapter 8:

Investing basics – common mistakes

Markets in recent times have become more complex, but also more volatile.

In simple words, the risk is increased. Economic factors, central bank interventions, negative rates, low inflation and algorithms are changing the equity, currency and commodity markets.

It seems that you no longer look at the fundamentals, but you buy the title of the moment and the one that presents a lower risk (in other words, people think it presents a lower risk).

In such difficult markets, small investors who invest in the stock market do not have an easy life. But this does not mean that they have to abandon the shares: with hard work and perseverance everyone can become a skilled investor.

To help you starting your journey, we have collected 15 of the most common mistakes beginner investors make. If you are able to avoid them, you will be one step ahead of the competition.

1. Relying on emotions

Most people lose on the stock market because they cannot manage their emotions.

It is proven that small savers buy in the upward phase of the markets, and panic sell at the first sign of decrease. Then what happens is that the market recovers, and they are now out.

This happens because of the poor financial education of the average American investor.

He who does not know how to assess the risk, does not know the diversification, and can't select the securities to put in the portfolio. He does not know how to calculate the average value of an asset.

He does not even know how to use a spreadsheet to calculate the volatility of a stock.

And it is precisely the lack of ability to manage the risk that will make him make bad decisions and will ultimately result in a loss.

2. Speculating, not investing

Another mistake that many often make is to confuse speculating with investing.

If you invest for the very short term, you increase the risk and it is not a question of investment but of speculation. Knowing how to define investment speculation is essential.

Before entering a title, you must define your time horizon and consider where to put the stop loss. One classical example of speculation is "binary options". They are often promoted as an investment, but they are not. For those who do not know what they are, binary options are bets placed on the price of an asset in the next 30 seconds. Yes, you read that right. Seriously, stay away from them.

3. Investing without planning

On the stock market, invested capital should not be necessary for daily life.

Before investing, plan these goals. Someone invests because in the future he wants to buy a bigger house. Others may invest for when they retire, but also for a holiday.

There are those who do it for their children. The real question is: why are you investing?

4. Thinking to be able to predict the future

What do Warren Buffet from Omaha and life coach Tony Robbins have in common? Both agree on the big risk that comes when our money is at stake.

During an interview with CNBC, Tony Robbins warned against a big mistake that is committed when it comes to investing for the future, which is, trying to predict the ups and downs of the market.

No one can predict the future, says Robbins, and legendary investors like billionaire Warren Buffett and Ray Dalio who is the founder of the titanic hedge fund Bridgewater Associates, tend to agree.

"Your plan for the future cannot be based on trying to time the market because you're going the wrong way."

Instead of buying and selling shares based on how small the small, Robbins suggests thinking long-term.

"You cannot afford to try and time the market. What we must do is study the long-term elements and have a diversification plan that protects when we are wrong ".

Buffett is also an important supporter of this type of strategy called "buy and hold", so much so that he wagered that the S & P 500 stock index would surpass hedge funds (which actively change investments). Now, it seems that most likely he will win that bet, which will bring him an extra $ 2 million in prize money.

Robbins also relies on the advice of Dalio, who founded the largest hedge fund in the world, Bridgewater Associates, which has difficulty identifying the right times to get in and out of investments. So, for Robbins, the best idea remains to look long-term and both he and Buffett suggest that they consider investing in low-cost index funds the best thing to do.

5. Not paying attention to costs

We have said it in all languages: costs can kill you financially. Investing € 15,000 for 30 years can result in € 106,000 capital if made with an ETF or a low-cost mutual fund, and € 67,000 if it is carried out with a mutual fund that has 2% of TER. See for yourself.

Realistically, saving costs is the only true "free money" that you can get as an investor. Financial products with high commissions are more often than not skylarks, just think of how overestimated Alfa's management idea is.

6. Changing the duration of the investment "on the go"

It usually works like this: you have chosen a portfolio assuming a certain duration of the investment, then the market "coughs", an instrument within the portfolio loses 5-6%, you read some negative opinions about it, start to shake like a rabbit and eventually sell. This change of time horizon does monstrous damages: typically, it makes you lose about half of the gains. Solution: invest a little at a time and do not think about it anymore.

7. Not diversifying

Diversification is useless only if you are able to predict the future and know what the best investment will be. If instead (as a normal human being) you do not have paranormal divinatory skills, you should diversify your portfolio a little but without exaggerating (more on that later).

8. Doing everything your broker says

If the bank, the promoter or the broker, push a product, run to check the costs: in 9 out of 10 cases it is the most convenient product for them and, as you can guess, the most expensive for you.

9. Not reading prospectuses and contracts well

By law, intermediaries are forced to write everything they do in a "contract" type of document. Often times, they will do it with that legal language that sends you into narcosis already in the second line. But you have to read everything, if you do not want bad surprises. Remember that you are responsible for your money and should not put the blame on others.

10. Buying unit-linked (and index-linked) policies

These policies are among the less transparent financial products that can be found, are padded with high commissions in favour of those who sell them. The seller will tell you a lot of nice stories about capital guarantee. Beyond the fantasies, with a unit-linked (or index-linked) policy, in 90% of cases you will have an expensive product, with severe penalties in case of early disinvestment and, after 10 or 20 years of payments, you will typically be rewarded with a disappointing performance (but console yourself, you will have made the man who sold it to you very happy).

11. Buying bonds from your bank

Bank bonds usually make less of a BTP of the same maturity, because they bear implicit charges like costs. Then, they are on average riskier and less liquid. And this is even true for subordinated bank bonds, whose holders, with the recent entry into force of the bail-in, are likely to be called to put their hands in the portfolio in the event of the issuer's default. Before buying these bonds, study them carefully, compare them with a governmental or supranational title (like BEI, BIS, etc.) and only then decide.

12. Believing to get rich with online trading

The colourful world of online trading is swarming with gurus to convince you that you will become rich thanks to their fabulous courses or their financial market forecasting site. Know that succeeding with trading is very difficult: in the vast majority of cases you will end up losing money and time. Learn to save and invest, not to trade.

13. Listening to economists, politicians and mass media

The noise in the ears distracts: eliminate it. So here is, for you and only for you, our personal list of noises that you have to get rid of.

- *Economists*. Think about how little they have put us in this story: for example, in 2009 they did not recognize the worst crisis since the Great Depression of 1929, in spite of a myriad of signals and, above all, the fact that the recession was already under its way.

- *Politicians*. Except for rare exceptions, the events of any Parliament are lively, full of funny and quarrelsome characters that combine all the colours, going from crisis to sudden solutions, and then plunge again into tragic crises: perfect plots for journalistic-television sagas. Generally, the impact on the financial markets of all this is low. For example, despite the ups and downs of Atalian politics, the spread has continued on its way, indifferent to everything but the ECB. Going on historical facts of weight, think that after the Japanese attack on Pearl Harbor in 1941 (which dragged the US into World War II) the stock index

Dow Jones lost only 6% (and in the following 12 months it gained 2,20%).

- *Mass-media*: newspapers, television. They bombard you with a continuous stream of news and data (often superficially explained), which lead you to deviate from your investment path (see point 2). Every day some economic data comes out: sometimes they improve, sometimes they get worse, but in the immediate future they rarely impact on your investments. Just to say, during the last recession in the Eurozone (which began in March 2012 and ended in June 2013), Eurozone stock markets have gained about 13%. So you focus on a few important things, check your wallet regularly, follow the right source of information, but do not be paranoid about the news.

14. Wanting to become successful over night

Do not be the investor who wants immediate success and who loses patience for daily highs and lows. Who wants quick results is certainly an example of how not to invest your savings if you want to succeed.

Investing successfully is a bit like taking care of a vegetable garden. Plants grow slowly, the first few years give little fruits, but then start to grow faster. In general, it is foolish to expect significant results in a few weeks, months or even in a few years. Remember that you do not want to get rich fast, you want to get rich for sure.

15. Not taking profits

It may seem strange, but there are lots of investors that never take out their profits. This is detrimental, since they never enjoy the money they earned through investing. It is like getting a gym subscription, but never going to the gym: it is useless and does not bring back to the practice.

The most successful investors always take out profits from time to time. Obviously, we are talking about calculated decisions and planned moves. However, the gold nugget here is the fact that if you do not have the money in your bank account, you cannot actually use it. It may sound silly, but it is a fact that most beginners tend to forget.

Chapter 9: How to choose a good stock to invest in

Since this is a guide for beginners and most people that start out decide to begin their investing journey with stocks, we thought it would be interesting to lay out the foundation of the topic. For those who choose to invest in stocks, the objective is undoubtedly that of obtaining the highest possible remuneration from their investment, which is why the choice of securities on which to invest their money is of fundamental importance.

Invest in stocks

In this regard, there are no universally valid and reliable rules that allow you to obtain good earnings and eliminate the risk of losses; otherwise the number of investors would be much higher.

In other words, the safe stocks to invest in, if they had ever existed in the past, today are officially extinct! However, this does not mean that plans cannot be made to reduce risk while maintaining a high level of profit.

Those who choose to invest in shares today are perfectly aware that there are a number of parameters that experts believe are essential to take into account when identifying the shares to be included in an investment portfolio. These parameters are: the capitalization of the company, the profitability of equity, the ratio between profit and price, the ratio of Ratio to price book value, the dividend yield and the ratings/target price. Let's see what these individual parameters consist of in detail, and how we can use them to choose the stocks to invest in today.

- *Capitalization of companies*: although this is a very often underestimated parameter, we must nevertheless consider that the size of the company is very often a sign of market power, in most cases through the possession of brands or technologies exploited globally. The use of this parameter, however, makes sense especially for equity investments in the US market, where over the last year companies with high capitalization (Apple, Coca Cola, Facebook, Google, Amazon, etc.) have seen a significant performance. The close relationship existing in the US shareholding between the level of capitalization on the stock exchange and the performance of the stock is one of the factors underlying the growing weight that American stocks have in the portfolios of international investors. The interest of traders in US stocks has also increased in light of the boom in listed companies operating in the tech and web segment.

- *Return over equity (Roe)*: this is the ratio between the net result and the net assets of a given company. In particular from the point of view of equity investments is an important parameter as profitability higher than the cost of capital is an index of the ability of an enterprise to create value. From this point of view the Roe is always held in strong consideration by those who choose to invest in shares today.

- *Price/earnings ratio*: a low ratio of this parameter makes a share price particularly attractive, but at the same time it could mean that expectations regarding future profits are not particularly positive. As in the case of the Roe this is a factor to be taken into consideration when choosing the best stocks to invest in.

- *Price/value ratio*: the ratio between the share price and the net asset value resulting from the last balance sheet, especially if this ratio is lower than the unit means that the company is being paid less than the value of the budget net of liabilities. However, this does not necessarily mean that it is a good deal, since the company may not be able to produce profits either.

- *Dividend yield*: this is the percentage ratio between the last distributed dividend and the share price, in particular it measures the remuneration provided by the company to shareholders in the last year in the form of liquidity. This parameter is often taken into account to identify the stocks to invest in, since a company able to distribute dividends is generally a healthy company, but also in this case, as with all the other selection parameters, it is necessary to make a broader and more complete analysis, since a high level of this indicator could also mean that the company has made few investments or has little prospect of growth. For this reason, looking at the dividend yield as a primary factor in determining the securities on which to invest in the stock market is reductive. The dividend yield only makes sense if accompanied by considerations on any business plans and industrial plans of the listed company. Only in this way is it possible to have guarantees on what are the prospects of the group in the future.

- *Rating and target price*: the rating is the judgement that certain analysts and investment banks have on a specific listed security while the target price represents the maximum target price to which the shares may reach. Dozens of judgements are published daily on all listed shares. Keeping an eye on these judgements is a way to have further clarification on what may be the prospects of the listed. If, in fact, more brokers decide to cut the rating on an X stock from buy to neutral or worse sell, then it means that, indeed, the expectations of the security in question are certainly not positive and therefore, perhaps, it is not the case to insert this title in the list of shares to invest in.

Clearly, promotions and failures (upgrades and downgrades) are not in the air but are accompanied by reports within which are explained the reasons behind that single judgement. Therefore, rating and target price are one of the most important factors for choosing the best stocks to invest in. As the great traders who focus on equities perfectly know, by looking at the history or the evolution of the rating and target price of a single stock, one can have an even more complete picture in the choice of actions to invest in today.

These are the main indicators that will dictate whether your investment will be successful or not. Taking time to study the structure of the company you want to invest in is extremely important, since it gives you the opportunity to get a better idea of where it is going and what it is aiming at for the future. Remember that when you invest in stocks, you own part of that project: it is your duty to fully understand it.

Here are some terms that you should familiarize with if you want to get better at stock investing.

Those who want to invest or play on the stock exchange, should consider or know some terms, which are basic for their trading actions. Some precautions must be taken into consideration:

- read constantly and daily, newspapers of an economic nature; this will mainly serve those who are not very familiar with the terminology used and consequently do not know the meaning of Actions, Bots, BTPs, Dow Jones, Nasdaq, Nikkei etc.

- Watch an economic news regularly, in such a way as to familiarize yourself and learn how to pronounce the most used terms;

- Document yourself through books, forums and online sites, this will greatly facilitate understanding and will also serve as a personal cultural baggage. In this way you can increase your knowledge and take your first steps in the world of economics.

A first term to know is certainly the word *share*, which is the cardinal element of the companies, which represents in all respects a share of the social capital of a company. The shares can be divided mainly into 3 categories:

- Ordinary shares: in which the holder can express his right to vote;

- Savings Shares: there is no possibility to cast a vote but give a greater dividend than previous shares;

- Preference Shares: guarantee "a greater privilege" in the allocation of profits and voting power in extraordinary shareholders' meetings.

During your investing journey, you will find yourself in contact with other important terms you should know. Some of the most popular ones are:

- BOTs, ordinary treasury bonds: they are issued in the short term and provide for a minimum subscription amount, which will be around € 1,000 and a return given by the difference between the repayment value and the purchase value;

- BTPs, multi-year Treasury bills: issued in the medium and long term, providing a fixed rate and a six-monthly coupon as a periodic earnings prospect for the security;

- CCT, Treasury credit certificates: issued in the medium and long term, and like the previous ones, these also provide for a six-monthly coupon with the addition of a yield indexed to that of the BOT;

- CTZ, zero coupon Treasury certificates: these provide for fixed rate securities, without a six-monthly coupon and have a variable maturity between 18 or 24 months.

- Dow Jones Index, of the American stock exchange that contains the thirty most important titles;

- Nasdaq, always referring to the American stock exchange and which contains the titles with high technological content;

- Nikkei, from the Japanese stock exchange. deals with the securities of the Japanese market;

- FTSE MIB, Financial Times Stock Exchange of Milan, inherent in the Italian stock exchange and concerns an average of the main Italian high capitalization securities;

- FTSE America Mid Cap, again the American stock exchange, including the securities of mid-cap companies;

- FTSE America Small Cap includes the small capitalization companies of the American stock exchange;

- MIB 30, contains the main American securities, and in particular the first 30 American companies;

- MIBTEL, an index that contains on a weighted average all the most important American titles.

Chapter 10:
How to invest big sums of money

This question would require a whole book to be eviscerated (and maybe I will write one about it in the near future), so it is more appropriate to warn you of the big mistakes that suggest fine operational details.

First of all, without a real competence it is quite absurd to throw yourself in too complicated things (for example high-risk long-term actions). Of course, you can get help from an expert, but then you can totally trust him. In this case it is useful to understand that, if not even a Nobel Prize for the economy can foresee profitable investments, how can a simple banking?

In economics too, many people sell expertise by exploiting favorable moments, except when the favourable moments are not ... to blame the astral conjunctures.

There is a famous saying that *economics is the second less reliable science, second only to astrology.*

In the real estate market, it is optimistic to hope to buy one or more houses and earn money automatically. It also takes a certain competence of the affair, a certain vision of the future (that is, of what is revalued and what does not, maybe because after ten years you build a landfill nearby) or (rents) you need to calculate the time from devote to the management of the property, taxes etc.

In the securities market it's even worse because so many beautiful tools delude you to make money.

The point is that who sells you a product is based on what happened in the past, without saying clearly that the past with the future has little to do with it (also because a few decades are not statistically significant to deduce something sensible). Not surprisingly, I do not know if you know, but in recent years it was really for a few to have a net gain, (ie removed inflation and management fees), many have simply ... lost.

Individual risks must also be mentioned: too many people invest a sum believing that they can withdraw at any moment (I marry, I have to buy the new house, the new car, I have to give a present to my son, etc.). That would result in disastrous repercussions. The "moment" always comes when your investments go down. The more one looks for a probable gain, the more he exposes himself to risks. Admitted and not granted that one can earn 2% net per year (ie over 20% in 10 years), in the ten years there may be a period of 2-3 years in which you are under 5%. If the "moment" of sales arrives in that period, to which it has been worth investing in a "smart" strategy. So, you can invest a lot, knowing that for 10 years you do not touch it and that you can touch it only if you are active. If you need substantial liquidity, you should not invest in medium to long-term choices.

Currently, if a person has a serious capital (ie that can lay still for a medium-long time) of less than 100,000 euros, it is better to invest only in safe and very short-term products, content with not losing on inflation. If capital is higher, it is convenient to become experts (but not those who delude themselves to break everything because funds, bonds and shares risk becoming the lottery of those who are only slightly more intelligent than others) or rely on a competent, realistic, and honest person. To skim the aspirants, try to ask what net gain a person can expect with x euro (shoot high): if you get an answer, "definitely at least y%" and y exceeds a few percentage points, forget it.

I wondered only if a person could have other income, in addition to those due to work.

Chapter 11:
How to decide if it is time to buy or sell a share

Indicators and graphs are one of the most important components when we talk about technical analysis. In addition to experience, coldness and psychology, a good analyst cannot disregard a thorough knowledge of the graphs. The latter can represent different information and may appear in different forms.

In graphical analysis, the graphs deserve particular attention because they represent the price dynamics of a given financial instrument and in a given period.

In the technical analysis the most commonly used type of graph is certainly the candle list chart, better known under the name of a Japanese candlestick chart. Before moving on to a detailed description of the candlestick chart, however, I would like to say a few words about two other charts, less used than candlestick charts, but which may be useful as they can help you understand the Japanese candlestick chart.

The price chart is shown on a Cartesian plane where, on the abscissa axis, that is the vertical axis the time is reported, while on the horizontal axis the price is reported.

Given this premise, we can still say that the graphs refer to different time periods whether they are fractions of minutes, hours and days, if not even weeks, months or even years indicating different sizes of opening or closing, of maximums and minima.

On the axis of the abscissas we find a space called histogram of the volume, which represents the quantity of instruments exchanged during the period under examination.

In graphic analysis in the specific and more generally in the technical analysis, various types of graph are used.

Features of a good chart

With the above, I do not mean that you will need a chart that contains a myriad of information or information in detail, but I would like to emphasize that the best successful traders on the market, use very few indicators. Yes, you understood correctly, only a few indicators. You will therefore think that what has been described up to now is only a chat, but it is not so, as these extrapolate the most important information directly from the graph. The charts obviously can only be provided by the brokers, which as for the forex market, here too we advise you to always choose the best binary options brokers. So it is not true that the graphics are all the same, it will be the good broker to extrapolate all the information that interests him from the various detailed charts. And from here we recognize the best brokers.

The reason for this extrapolation is very simple: since the indicators express only the past in a graphic form, they can provide a very approximate vision of the future. Therefore, too many indicators in a chart can sometimes create confusion instead of clarity and aid.

Therefore, we consider very important to keep the following points in mind:

1. Good graphic program.

With this in fact you should always be able to look far enough in the past, to plan the future and identify relevant barriers and gather a satisfactory overview. In the binary options charts of the different brokers this time frame is too narrow to draw reliable conclusions.

2. Good quality graphs always indicate different time intervals.

These range from a few minutes to a maximum of a month.

3. Never set just a common linear chart.

This fact would not be very useful for technical analysis purposes. On the other hand, candle or beam charts are used, which we will explain briefly.

What is chart analysis?

The analysis of the graphs is above all the search for particular shapes, also called graphic structures, configurations or figures.

They are figures that emerge from the price movement, and that can signal its future trend. They are tracked by analysts joining points in the price graph of a financial security or the performance of an indicator.

The purpose of the graphic analysis will therefore be to identify the most typical price patterns for forecasting purposes.

These graphic formations can be classified into different categories. The main categories of classes can assume inversion or continuation or consolidation characteristics. Fundamental feature will also be the dynamics of the volumes, which we will explain under each figure.

This is why it takes technique, experience, strategies, if not the analyst's ability to see these forms in the movement of a graph. These are the fundamental elements of this type of analysis. The concept of trendline, support and resistance are also part of this aspect of technical analysis.

Below we will list the most used graphs for graphic analysis and explain the operation. Before doing this, however, we must explain another very important and used concept: the figure of Continuation. These have common characteristics in all the graphs; they represent a pause in the prevailing trend in progress and are a prelude to a continuation of the trend in the direction of the direction previously underway. For this reason they are also known as consolidation figures.

The main difference between the continuation and the inversion figures concerns the extension.

The continuation figures are often accompanied by a decrease in the volumes traded.

One of the first figures we are going to examine is the wedge.

Wedge

This too is a continuation figure on explained and is very similar to the triangle for 2 reasons:

- For the form;

- For the time it takes to form. This differs from the triangle that we will see below, because the shape that forms is characterized by a strongly bullish or bearish inclination opposite to that of the current trend.

This means that:

- this chart consists of two convergent trendlines and takes about one to three months to develop;
    - in an uptrend, a falling wedge or "a descending wedge" can be encountered;
    - while in a bearish tendency a rising wedge or "an ascending wedge" can develop.

As with the pennant and flag figures, the wedge can be found in the middle of a movement, thus allowing us to calculate minimum targets.

The dynamics of the volumes sees a decrease in the course of the formation of the pattern and it should go to be reduced for all the period of formation of the figure. On the contrary, they increase significantly when the trendline is broken, which is a typical feature of the wedge.

The second figure we examine in this chapter is the pennant.

Pennant

This figure is also quite common in chart analysis.

This figure together with the figure of the flag, which we will see immediately after the flag appears after an almost vertical movement and represents a pause in the trend.

Its characteristic is that it is presented as a symmetrical triangle which, however, has a maximum extension of 3 weeks. Most often in bearish actions the refinement time of the figure is even lower and is equal to one or maximum two weeks. The pennant is halfway to the bullish or bearish movement, with the obvious implications in calculating the minimum targets for the movement's arrival.

It will therefore be obvious that the volume decreases during the formation of the figure and should be low throughout the period of formation of the pattern. On the contrary, instead, they increase significantly when the trendline breaks, which identifies the pennant. These are accompanied by a similar trend in the range within which prices move.

Pennants most often coincide with a contraction phase, which does not necessarily have an opposite inclination with respect to the basic trend.

Both this figure and the next develop within a rather short time frame.

The third figure that we examine as announced is the Flag.

Flag

Flag formation, or flag, is a very common pattern of continuation in graphic analysis.

This form tends to appear close to the temporary exhaustion of a trend, which represents a brief pause in the market after strongly accentuated movements, are almost vertical and known as flagpole.

The flag has a shape similar to a parallelepiped, almost to represent a rectangle, bounded by two parallel trendlines but opposed to the prevailing trend.

In other words, it can be seen as a flag that is tilted downward in an uptrend and upward in a bearish trend.

His training ends within a medium period, that is, between one and three weeks. It usually appears halfway to complete movement.

It must also be said that if it is in a bearish movement the perfection time is less and the figure is usually completed in one or two weeks. Precisely because it is in the middle of the bullish or bearish movement, the figure is important for identifying price targets. From here we will then calculate the width of the movement preceding the flag and report this distance after the break of the tread line delineating the figure.

The volume should also decrease during the formation of the figure and then increase again when the trendline is broken.

So, let's see how to use Flag and Pennant.

The targets that can be identified in relation to these figures are two:

- The first is determined by projecting the width of the base from the breakout point; here this target assumes less importance, if we consider the reduced dimensions of the figure.

- The second can instead be obtained by projecting, from the breakout point, a distance equivalent to that covered by the movement that preceded the formation of the pennant.

- This means that these figures often materialize around half of the overall movement, giving a fair advantage at the operational level.

The temporary phase of price weakness can be exploited to enter the stock or even just to increase the position taken earlier, again using a stop-loss much lower than the potential take-profit.

The fourth figure that we will explain will be represented by the rectangle.

Rectangle

The rectangle is the simplest among the figures proposed by the technical analysis.

It identifies a phase of price congestion. In Technical Analysis, with this term we mean a graphic formation in correspondence with which prices oscillate within a narrow range of values. This process takes place when the market moves sideways.

The pattern represents a break zone of the current trend in which prices move sideways. This also gives rise to the name of trading range or congestion area, a figure that represents a period of consolidation of the current trend that is resolved in the direction of the trend that preceded it. This represents a fundamental figure, to correctly identify the continuation pattern if not also the observation of the volumes.

Also, for this bullish figure the rebounds must be accompanied by high volumes, with the corrections characterized by decreasing volumes. In the opposite case, instead, in the bearish rectangle, are the corrections to have more accentuated volumes.

Many investors, take advantage of the oscillations, selling to the top of the figure and buying at the minimum. However, those who use this approach risk not exploiting the breaking of the pattern.

The figure in question usually takes from one to three months to improve and the minimum target is represented by the translation of the height of the rectangle when the price breaks the figure.

Prices move within a fixed band identified by a support and resistance as better shown in the figure below.

First target 1

The rectangles can also be configured as inversion figures, depending on the context in which they are formed. It is therefore evident how the congestion phases identify a moment in which the market expresses considerable uncertainty and awaits new information to decide the future trend. Unlike the contraction phases (in which the continuous reduction in volatility identifies in an increasingly precise manner the moment in which the market will receive the information that waits) a figure of congestion like the rectangle does not allow to identify sufficiently in advance the moment in which the breakout will take place.

The operational cues that this figure can provide are basically of two types:

- The first requires waiting for the exit of prices from the congestion zone initially identified. This exit must necessarily be classified as a breakout and therefore must be characterized by an increase in volumes and volatility.

- The second operational step derives from the possibility of exploiting the lateral movement of prices to buy close to the identified support and sell when the values are near the top of the figure again.

Support and Resistance

Let me now explain briefly what the supports and the resistances are.

Support is defined as that price level at which there is, an arrest of the downward trend in prices. An excessive concentration of purchases that occurs in the vicinity of the same will cause a block in the downward trend in prices.

A level of support is defined as reliable when it shows resistance to repeated "attacks" without a bearish breakdown.

The Resistance is defined instead as that level of price where the growth of the same stops. In the case of the Resistance, the high concentration of sales prevents the continuation of the increase.

A resistance level, on the contrary, is stronger and more reliable as it resists repeated "attacks" without an upward failure.

Surely a historical minimum or maximum represents a level of Support or Strategic Resistance.

Consequently, the penetration or breaking of support levels or even resistance can be caused by:

- important changes in the fundamental values of a company (increase in profits, changes in management, etc.);

- from simple forecasts based on price trends in recent times; and

- both levels of support and resistance can also arise from motivations exclusively of an emotional nature. Supports and resistances represent with great simplicity the encounter/clash between supply and demand.

From the above it is clear that in practice, a breakout, or an event in which the price comes out of a trend, breaking a support or resistance or a channel, above a level of resistance evidence an increase in demand, arising from more buyers, who are willing to buy at higher prices than the current ones.

In the opposite case, instead, the breakdown of a support shows an increase in the sellers, and therefore in the offer, as more sellers are willing to sell even at lower prices than the current ones.

If a level of support is broken, it automatically turns into a resistance level, just as if a resistance level is broken; it becomes a level of support. This process is known as pullback, which is a time when a trending market takes a break.

The support and resistance lines can be drawn horizontally and then we will talk about static support, where the support corresponds to a precise and constant point in time; both obliquely and in this case, we will talk about dynamic support, where a trendline is drawn with the variation of prices and with the passage of time.

The fifth figure, object of study, concerns the triangle.

Triangle

In technical analysis, that of the triangle is a consolidation figure and is used to verify the continuation of the main trend. This is a pattern that lasts a few months when there is a pause in the current trend with prices that oscillate in an increasingly narrow area.

The figure has the following characteristics:

The triangle must have a minimum of four reaction points; two superiors, and two inferiors; the first ones necessary to trace the upper trendline, the seconds necessary to draw the lower trend line.

The triangle is characterized by a time limit for its resolution. Usually the prices break the triangle at a point between two thirds and three quarters of the depth of the triangle.

The volumes in the formation phase of the triangle waves lose strength and then explode when the trendline that delimits the figure breaks.

The minimum target for price trends is calculated by projecting the maximum height of the triangle.

The figure in question can present itself according to three different structures:

- symmetrical triangle which has the trendlines that delimit it that are convergent.

Prices tend to move in a range that gradually becomes narrower with the passing of the sessions, due to a constant reduction of the maximums, and also due to a constant reduction of the minimums.

- descending triangle characterized by a flat demarcation line, the lower one, and by a bearish trend line, the upper one.

In this figure there will be a greater conviction on the part of the bearish and is often found during a downward trend.

The reduction in the range within which prices move, occurs only thanks to an increase in the minimum, while the maximums remain almost unchanged.

Just such behavior makes evident the greater pressure of the buyers with respect to the sellers and attributes to this figure a bullish value.

Descending Triangle

The figure represents a symmetrical structure, which makes it difficult to interpret. In the third case, on the other hand, we speak of an ascending triangle, characterized by an upper line of flat demarcation and a line, the lower, ascending line. This pattern indicates a greater strength of the uptrend and is often found during an uptrend

Regardless of the configuration, whether symmetrical, ascending or descending, it is possible to calculate the target of the figure, like the level that prices should reach in the phase following the breakout.

This is calculated by projecting, from the breaking point, the "base" of the triangle, like the maximum width that the figure recorded during its formation.

The sixth figure in question concerns the formation of broadening.

Broadening

This represents a rather rare figure, classified as a variant of the triangle but which presents a contrary opening, with divergent trendlines. It is a figure that occurs at the end of a trend, usually bullish.

The dynamics of the volumes are different from that of the triangles, as the volume gradually expands together with the increase in price oscillation.

The seventh figure that we are going to examine concerns the diamond.

Diamond

Also, the diamond as an inversion figure is one of the rarest and one of the least simple to detect. Graphically the diamond is formed by a double figure composed of a first half that recalls the shape of a broadening from a second half that resembles a symmetrical triangle.

A diamond can present itself in two circumstances:

- at the end of an uptrend; and

- at the end of a bearish trend.

In the first case it takes the name of "Diamond Top", vice versa we would be facing a "Diamond Bottom".

The figure does not always develop symmetrically. Often, the second half is prolonged in time more than the first one did.

By its nature the diamond needs very dynamic market phases. The figure of the Diamond can also occur during simple breaks of the trend.

For this reason, it is easier to find the diamond at the peak of an upward trend before a bearish reversal rather than the other way round.

The dynamics of volumes go hand in hand with that of prices. That is, if volumes increase, prices increase, in the second half, however, prices fall and consequently also volumes.

There are 4 basic elements to identify the training:

an initial phase of price expansion;

a maximum;

a minimum;

a phase of price contraction;

The pattern is only complete when the support or resistance line breaks and a pullback to the violated trendline do not always occur.

The minimum price target is equal to the maximum vertical distance between the two extreme parts of the figure projected at the bottom (or at the top) with respect to the breaking point of the support or resistance.

It is possible, even for the diamond, to calculate a target price.

It is sufficient to project the maximum width of the figure and project starts from the point where the breakout occurred.

In the event that it is configured as a continuation figure, it is also possible to derive a second target, projecting the width of the movement that preceded the beginning of the diamond, from the point of the final breakout (diamond breaking points)

The eighth figure we examine will be a figure difficult enough to examine and represents the rounding and spike.

Rounding and Spike

This represents one of the many figures of inversions, which presents itself as a slow and gradual movement on the lows that will first have a slight downward, then lateral and then shows a growing movement.

The pattern is one of the slowest of all the graphic analysis and is usually identifiable on longer term charts.

It is really difficult to establish the precise moment in which the figure can be considered complete, if not after the first substantial rises. Even more difficult, it will be to identify upward targets.

Spike is also very special. The figures in question show, without any transition period, a sudden reversal of the quotations. An inversion accompanied by an explosion of volumes.

Due to its characteristics, the figure in question is difficult to identify in advance.

Double Top and Double Bottom

Also, this falls into the categories of the inversion figures, which we remember are particular graphic figures that announce an inversion of the current trend. The figure in question turns out to be a very common figure in graphic analysis and together with other figures, the double bottom and double top figures are among the most common and recognizable formations.

We explain briefly in two essential steps, its operation;

1. The double minimum is at the peak of a bearish trend and is configured as a minimum, a subsequent rebound and a subsequent fall back to the level of the previous minimum. The ascent that follows, if it breaks on the upside and with volumes the previous maximum, leads to the completion of the figure. The pattern, due to its shape, is also called a formation in W. Volumes are growing during the formation of the first minimum, down in the following rebound, and then increase again during the upward movement that completes the figure.

Basically, therefore, the double minimum is realized, following a clear bearish trend, in which prices test twice a price threshold, but without being able to overcome it. This determines the realization of two minimums slightly spaced over time, double minimum and double maximum.

2. Also, the characteristics of the double maximum are the same, but the pattern has a secularly opposite development. The double top is at the height of an

uptrend and is configured as a maximum, a consequent fall and a subsequent rebound towards the previous maximum.

The double maximum is achieved when, following a sharp uptrend, prices test twice a price threshold, but without being able to overcome it, determining the formation of two maximums. Volumes are growing at the formation of the first rise, remaining lower in the formation of the second maximum and then increasing conspicuously at the time of the piercing of the traceable line starting from the previous minimum.

In both figures it is possible to observe a return of prices to the level of completion of the pattern, in a pullback similar to that of the head and shoulders that we will see later, before the definitive start of the new trend, bullish in the double minimum and bearish in the double maximum. This pullback is accompanied by small volumes.

The measurement of the minimum upward (or downward) target is calculated by calculating the distance between the line joining the two minima (or the two maxima) and the first maximum (or minimum) relative and projecting this value from the upward drilling point or downward.

In essence, the double minimum or the double maximum is however a graphic formation with a degree of reliability lower than other figures of inversion, both because it is not always detectable with sufficient certainty, and because it often occurs in conditions of volatility so high that allow identification of a valid breakout.

Triple Top and Triple Bottom

The triple maximum and the triple minimum are also inversion figures, defined as variants of the head and shoulders, but unlike the previous ones, the three maxima and the three minima are all placed at the same height.

The volumes to be considered, in the triple minimum correspond to each rise, starting from a minimum is accompanied by decreasing volumes. The pattern is completed when the line obtained by joining the last maximum with extremely high volumes is breached upwards, triple maximum

In the triple maximum, any downward correction starting from a maximum is accompanied by declining volumes, and consequently the figure can be said to be complete, when the level obtained by joining the last lows is violated downwards with volumes in great growth. In the triple minimum, however, the minimum target is common to that used for head and shoulders, a figure that we will see shortly if not also equal to double minimum and double maximum, based on the height of the figure.

Head and Shoulders

This is also an inversion figure and is one of the most reliable graphic patterns. According to some authors, the figure in question is the most powerful among all those found on a chart.

In a graph head and shoulders consist of three consecutive increases, interspersed with two bearish inversions. The second rise is generally more robust than the others and represents the heads. The first and third instead represent the shoulders and are less pronounced than the head. The completion of the figure is obtained by perforating the line, joining the two reaction minima, called Neck-line. The logic that underlies the formation is simple. The price cannot confirm its strength, it does not create new highs and the trend deteriorates. The succession of rising highs and lows, a fundamental dynamic to define an uptrend, is conditioned.

During the first phase there is the formation of a maximum accompanied by volatility and high volumes. After a partial retracement prices make a new maximum, however, registering a reduction in volumes. After a new retracement the prices make a new relative maximum, lower than the previous one and accompanied by reduced volumes. The completion of the figure requires the breakout of the neckline, which coincides with the straight line that unites the two points in which the prices have partially retraced (2 and 4). At the breakout the volatility and volumes return to be high. The breakout moment can then be followed by a pullback, that is, price return movement close to the neckline (which, in this phase, will assume the role of resistance).

The line that joins the base formed by the two reaction minima is fundamental. This line is also called "neckline", or its neckline, and its importance derives from the fact that the figure is completed only when the price drills this level downwards.

The neckline is usually horizontal or inclined in the same direction as the trend to be reversed. In this last case it has greater value.

Usually, after the neckline is broken, there is a movement of prices returning towards the neckline itself, in a dynamic called "pullback". If the prices fail to return above the neckline, confirmation of the perfection of the figure is complete.

Operationally it is possible to close the long positions at the rupture of the uptrend trendline that unites the upward minimums on the downside of the head but before opening any short positions a sharp break of the neckline is expected.

The "head and shoulders" can be configured both as a bearish figure and as a bullish figure: in the second case the three maxima described above will be replaced by three minimums, but the evolution of the figure - also from the point of view of volumes and volatility - it will remain the same. The target can be calculated by projecting the width of the figure (coinciding with the distance between the "head" and the neckline) from the breakout point. Among the inversion figures, the "head and shoulders" is perhaps the one that - once completed - provides the greatest degree of reliability, determining the achievement of the target in a rather short time..

In the development of a head and shoulders the dynamics of the volumes is a fundamental aspect. The three maxima, the left shoulder, the head and the right shoulder, must have low volumes. To give a stronger confirmation to the perfection of the figure the neckline rupture should instead occur with volumes in explosion, while those of the possible pullback should be again decreasing with an increase in the subsequent downward movement.

The reputation of the head and shoulders is also due to its ability to give the chart analyst precise price targets, a feature that allows us to know already at the time of entry into position which will be the likely gains of the operation but also what will be the related risks. The stop losses necessary to defend their investments can also be positioned.

We therefore see that the first minimum target is given by the downward projection of the calculable distance between the neckline and the vertex of the head while the second target is obtained by adding to the first target the extension of the right shoulder.

The head and shoulder variant is the inverted shoulder head, a powerful inversion figure that can be found on the market minimums and at the end of a bearish or bullish trend. The figure in question, is formed by three consecutive minima, where the second minimum is more extensive than the first and third. Also, in this case, the current trend deteriorates between the head and the right shoulder.

The result is a lack of the main characteristic of a bearish tendency, that is, that of the alternation between lower and higher declines.

Chapter 12: Indicators to look for before investing

Traders and investors in the stock market use different techniques to choose the securities to invest in. Some make greater use of technical analysis, others of fundamental analysis.

To choose the stock to invest in, especially if you intend to do it for a medium-long period, it is good to use both types of analysis.

The fundamental analysis makes it possible to evaluate a stock, thus understanding the real underlying value of the action. Technical analysis, on the other hand, allows us to understand which the best entry is and exit points from a stock and often reflects the evaluation of the fundamental analysis.

Furthermore, by combining the two types of market analysis, one can not only analyse the graphs, but also study the historical trend of an investment.

It is in fact important to know both the price trend at the time when you are trading and understand the changes in the past.

In this chapter, we illustrate the fundamental analysis parameters to be taken into account when choosing a stock and you will see how technical analysis can help you to climb up or down the price of an action.

Here's how to choose a stock to invest in.

As anticipated, it is preferable, in the stock market, to use both analyses, because together they provide a clearer picture for the choice of a stock.

Starting from the fundamental analysis, the parameters on which to base for the choice of a title are the following:

- ROE and ROA (or ROI)
- the price / earnings ratio (P / E) and EPS (earnings per share)
- the price / value ratio of the book (P / BV)
- news, management quality and visibility of the title.

Let's look at each of these aspects in detail, so as to create a complete content that can guide even the less experienced in choosing actions.

The stock exchange operator who compares with the stock market to choose a stock initially looks to ROE (Return on Equity). This financial indicator offers the trader the opportunity to evaluate the rate of return on equity, ie the part of the financial statements that remunerates shareholders.

High levels of ROE, both current and future, indicate that the company issuing the security is able to guarantee a high return for investors.

However, the only use of ROE can be misleading as it does not take into account the level of indebtedness. By definition, equity is the difference between total assets and liabilities.

If liabilities rise, the denominator of the ROE will tend to decrease, pushing the overall value upwards. Operators then typically compare ROE with ROA (Return on Assets) which tells us how profitable the company's assets are.

High ROE and ROA values indicate that the ROE growth is truthful as the [ROA] takes into account the liabilities in the denominator that as the number increases, it will tend to increase, thus compressing the percentage of ROA.

The P / E and the EPS

Together with the ROE and the ROA, we also look at the P / E and the EPS. The P / E is the ratio between the stock price and EPS, like the profit generated by the company for each outstanding share.

The P / E falls into the category of "comparable", those parameters that can be compared with those of similar or sector companies. Some operators tend to compare the P / E of a company with that of the sector but making a mistake.

In fact, we cannot compare the P / E with the simple mathematical average of the reference sector, since the latter includes P / E of companies which, by structure and profitability, are not similar to that analysed.

It is therefore good to compare the P / E with that of similar companies rather than the average sector. So, when you do your analysis, be careful not to fall into this trap.

The EPS instead is the denominator of the P / E. If the P / E falls while the EPS rises is the ideal situation (assuming that ROE and ROA are optimal).

This is because it indicates that the share price is not reflecting earnings growth, thus showing an underestimation of the market on the security in question.

The P / BV

To give further proof of the goodness of the analysis, the P / BV intervenes (price/book value). If the ROE grows structurally well (like that there are no deviations caused by the increase in debt) and the P / BV is low there is a further suggestion of underestimating the stock to be chosen.

This is because the price is not absorbing the growth of the book value (equity) which is the part of the balance sheet that interests the stock investor.

The scheme to choose

To summarize, then, the fundamental analysis formula that allows the optimal choice of a stock is:

Current and prospective high ROE and ROA;

- P / E relatively low compared to competitors and EPS growing;

- Low P / BV (also comparable with sector competitors)

News impact

Another point that concludes the fundamental analysis of a stock is the news circulating on the issuing company and on the market sentiment towards management. If we choose to invest in a stock, it is good to take a look at recent company news.

Positive news generally reflects the sentiment of the market on the company, which is a good sign for future increases in the security in question. Evaluating management skills is also a good idea because if the leaders of the company are positively perceived by the market, this will have a positive attitude towards the choices of managers and especially towards the stock.

Finally, consider where the stock is listed. If we are talking about small-cap companies, in phases of the market that are not at risk, the title cannot be higher. This is because the shares listed on smaller indices enjoy less visibility because of the inclusion on indices of lesser importance.

All this then over 3 months, this is because the methodology illustrated applies well to medium but also fairly short periods. Finally, look at the degree of correlation of the security in question with the benchmark index, comparing the relative strength of the stock to be chosen with that of the price list.

If the stock shows relative strength to the index, it means that the stock we are choosing has a trend untied from that of the reference index, which indicates that its strength is safe even in times that are not optimal in the index of quotation.

Chapter 13:
How to diversify your investment

A valid question all investors ask themselves. After all, we must start from another question: why is it important to diversify your investments? Simple: to reduce risks. It goes without saying that investing in several different assets involves a better distribution of risk. So, if for example an action is at a loss, we will always have the hope that a precious metal is on the rise instead.

Below we will try to offer a comprehensive picture on how to diversify your investments, thus better understanding why it is important to diversify your investments.

Why is it important to diversify? We have said that this practice is useful for reducing investment risks. The world today is globalized, so even the stock exchanges are connected to each other in an extreme way. Therefore, the crisis of an exchange carries with it all the others. Furthermore, today's World, especially since the 1990s with the collapse of the Berlin Wall, has become economically very variable and unpredictable. The logic that drives diversification responds to the impossibility of knowing in advance the future performance of our investments. A variable in which, substantially, the risk of each investment lies. The basic idea to minimize the risks deriving from this uncertainty consists in splitting its investments into different projects, thus spreading the risk linked to the performance of individual investments.

Moreover, each asset is linked to multiple variables. For example, actions are closely related to a company's performance, which often, also hides its real financial situation. Such as in agricultural raw materials, in which a bacterium destroys the crop causing a collapse. Regarding the extraction of oil, just the disaster of a platform or a strike of the workers to cause the collapse of the flock and what about a coup or unexpected election results.

How to diversify your investments?

Before finding an answer, it is necessary to understand that investments are divided into 5 large areas:

1. Stock

Area consisting of all shares, funds, ETFs, individual securities

2. Real estate

This area includes financial instruments related to real estate

3. Commodities

For commodities we mean all those products mainly related to the soil, then cultivable. Like coffee, cocoa, sugar, soy, wheat. But also, to the subsoil, like the energy fields like oil, gas and so on.

4. Precious metals

Precious metals include, as you can guess, gold, silver and platinum.

5. Bonds

Bonds include both government securities and bonds issued by private companies.

Investing means making precise choices and selecting one asset rather than another. If I invest in share ownership, it means that I am deducting money from the other 4 markets.

However, it should always be kept in mind that money is something unfaithful. Because if today it is aimed at a type of investment, tomorrow it will move towards another. So, if today precious metals are good, tomorrow will sooner or later go to the raw materials. For tomorrow, obviously, we mean after a few years. So it's like a few years' engagement.

But when he changes partners, he ends up betraying billions of people who believed in that area of investment. And every time it's a severe blow, because the values collapse

History is full of such betrayals. In 2007, for example, it happened to properties and shares. And the latter collapsed in 2000 as well. In 1980, however, it was the turn of gold. Of course, the stories of love are also prolonged, like that of the stock market started in 1984 and came up to 2000. Or like the one started in 2000 up to 2007 on real estate. Recently, however, money seems to have become attached to precious metals.

Therefore, money moves cyclically and even if it may "fall in love" with more investment areas, it will do so more clearly towards an area. How to defend oneself from the volatility of the market? Surely inquire and train as much as possible, reading the economic news, taking a look at the countries on which to invest (considering their economic and political stability for example) or growing companies. Then it is advisable to rely on a trusted financial advisor to build your portfolio together.

What are the best assets to diversify your investments? Experts generally place MTB (acronym of multi-year Treasury Bonds) in first place, although the state coupons market is constantly evolving. In this historical moment, it is preferable to invest small amounts over the long term. However, it is worth stressing that these securities remain the safest investment to date, allowing a regular withdrawal of coupons with returns.

If instead we want faster and more substantial results, then the stock market is recommended for us. However, it must be said that large returns also correspond to much higher investment risks. So, we have to ponder perfectly how much to invest and on which institutions or companies. The properties are still to be avoided, since, after the bubble of the last decade, they have lost value. Although, it should also be added that the market believes that when the price falls it is just the right time to buy. Just to get a regular monthly entry through rent. Or sell when the market is bullish again.

Bonds are another alternative but must be "guaranteed" and not subject to the performance of the companies to which they are affiliated. Finally, gold is always a good refuge, just like other precious materials or valuable paintings.

How to diversify our investments through ETF? Many investors believe, naively, that it is enough to increase the number of investments to improve the diversification of the portfolio. But this is a dangerous simplification. If we invest our savings in individual securities, be they stocks or bonds, the number of products to be included in the portfolio must be raised to minimize the risk associated with each of the investments made.

On the other hand, if we invest our savings in active mutual funds, or passive funds such as ETFs, we can achieve great diversification by reducing the number of instruments. Each fund (or ETF) is in fact a container of financial instruments, so with a few products we can actually divide our portfolio into hundreds of different securities.

The main features of ETFs are:

- passive management
- their listing on the stock exchange as shares and bonds

With the former it is intended that their return is closely linked to the listing of a stock exchange index and not to the fund manager's buying and selling ability. The stock index may be equity, commodity, bond, monetary, or other. The manager's job is limited to checking the consistency of the fund with the benchmark index. But also correct the value in the event of deviations. The difference between the price of the fund and that of the benchmark index is in the order of 1 or 2%.

"Passive management" therefore makes ETFs very cheap, to which is added their large or huge diversification, and their stock trading. All this makes them competitive compared to investing in individual stocks and less risky. However, there is also a lack of speculative level, inverted, or reversed leverage. ETFs are very convenient as they allow investing in many economic sectors: liquidity, bond indices, geographic equity markets, commodities, commodity sectors.

Example of diversification of investments

Suppose we have a capital to invest of 500 euros. And so we decide to diversify investments in equal parts among the 5 assets. Now let's say that for each asset the trend was as follows:

Stocks: + 7%

Properties: - 6%

Commodities: - 10%

Precious metals: + 21%

Bonds: + 3%

Now, by making a calculation on the 100 euros invested per asset, we will have the following results: € 107 + € 94 + € 90 + € 121 + € 103 = € 515 total

We will therefore have earned € 15 or 3% on our initial invested capital. How is our result to be considered? It depends on our ambitions. If we play not to lose, then we will surely be satisfied. If we are traders who are content with little, we will be satisfied. If instead we do a more general calculation, perhaps considering an increase in personal expenses during the year, etc., then we will have a half reaction: we have not lost but not earned as well. If instead we are expert traders, then that 3% will appear miserable to us. Finally, if we are traders who want to push our earnings, then we will be completely dissatisfied. And we will think that perhaps having invested only in precious metals would have earned us 605 euros.

All this to say that the answer to the question of our satisfaction or not depends on us, from our ambitions but of course, also from our formation. In fact, if we are beginners, then it is clear that for fear we will tend to equally distribute our money. But if we have the right experience and training on the subject, we will have the nose to invest on one or two assets only and those we will consider to be the winning ones.

Conclusion

Thank for making it through to the end of *Stock Market Investing for Beginners: Simple Proven Strategies and Tactics to become a Profitable Intelligent Investor by getting hold of the tricks behind the trade toward success and fortune,* let's hope it was informative and able to provide you with all of the tools you need to achieve your financial goals.

The next step is to begin to apply what you have learned during the course of this book and get started right away. Our suggestion is always to open up a demo account on a broker and make a few tries, before putting real money into it. Remember that you should never risk more than what you can afford to lose, so manage your capital wisely.

We hope that you find these lessons valuable and that you got the information you were looking for. Letting your money work for you will give you an incredible feeling, especially at the beginning, when you make the first gains. We are thrilled for you to start and we cannot wait to see your results coming in.

www.ingramcontent.com/pod-product-compliance
Ingram Content Group UK Ltd.
Pitfield, Milton Keynes, MK11 3LW, UK
UKHW022225230426
12048UKWH00016BA/1072